New Directions for
Student Services

Elizabeth J. Whitt
EDITOR-IN-CHIEF

John H. Schuh
ASSOCIATE EDITOR

Gender and Sexual Diversity in U.S. Higher Education: Contexts and Opportunities for LGBTQ College Students

Dafina-Lazarus Stewart
Kristen A. Renn
G. Blue Brazelton

EDITORS

Number 152 • Winter 2015
Jossey-Bass
San Francisco

GENDER AND SEXUAL DIVERSITY IN U.S. HIGHER EDUCATION: CONTEXTS AND OPPORTUNITIES FOR LGBTQ COLLEGE STUDENTS
Dafina-Lazarus Stewart, Kristen A. Renn, G. Blue Brazelton (eds.)
New Directions for Student Services, no. 152

Elizabeth J. Whitt, Editor-in-Chief
John H. Schuh, Associate Editor

NEW DIRECTIONS FOR STUDENT SERVICES (ISSN 0164-7970, e-ISSN 1536-0695) is part of The Jossey-Bass Higher and Adult Education Series and is published quarterly by Wiley Subscription Services, Inc., A Wiley Company, at Jossey-Bass, One Montgomery Street, Suite 1200, San Francisco, CA 94104-4594. POSTMASTER: Send address changes to New Directions for Student Services, Jossey-Bass, One Montgomery Street, Suite 1200, San Francisco, CA 94104-4594.

New Directions for Student Services is indexed in CIJE: Current Index to Journals in Education (ERIC), Contents Pages in Education (T&F), Current Abstracts (EBSCO), Education Index /Abstracts (H.W. Wilson), Educational Research Abstracts Online (T&F), ERIC Database (Education Resources Information Center), and Higher Education Abstracts (Claremont Graduate University).

Microfilm copies of issues and articles are available in 16 mm and 35 mm, as well as microfiche in 105 mm, through University Microfilms Inc., 300 North Zeeb Road, Ann Arbor, Michigan 48106-1346.

SUBSCRIPTIONS cost $89 for individuals in the U.S., Canada, and Mexico, and $113 in the rest of the world for print only; $89 in all regions for electronic only; and $98 in the U.S., Canada, and Mexico for combined print and electronic; and $122 for combined print and electronic in the rest of the world. Institutional print only subscriptions are $335 in the U.S., $375 in Canada and Mexico, and $409 in the rest of the world; electronic only subscriptions are $335 in all regions; and combined print and electronic subscriptions are $402 in the U.S., $442 in Canada and Mexico, and $476 in the rest of the world.

EDITORIAL CORRESPONDENCE should be sent to the Editor-in-Chief, Elizabeth J. Whitt, University of California Merced, 5200 North Lake Rd. Merced, CA 95343.

Cover design: Wiley
Cover Images: © Lava 4 images | Shutterstock

www.josseybass.com

CONTENTS

In this final chapter, the editors revisit the key ideas and points raised in the preceding chapters and outline recommendations for research, policy, and practice to effect transformative change in higher education for LGBTQ students.

Editors' Notes

Accompanying the trajectory of campus and community activism for visibility and civil rights, research on the experiences and identities of lesbian, gay, bisexual, transgender, and queer (LGBTQ) college students has grown from a few small studies in the 1990s to a robust literature that supports educational policy and programs. A 2005 *New Directions for Student Services* sourcebook on gender identity and sexual orientation (Sanlo, 2005) brought together the latest scholarship of that time on identity development, campus climate and policies, transgender issues, and institutional features such as type, leadership, and campus resources. Since 2005 researchers have widened their lens to include, among other topics, LGBTQ student engagement and success, and they have focused their lens on specific topics such as transgender identity development and understanding intersections of sexual orientation and gender identity with other salient identities such as faith/religion/spirituality, race, social class, and ability. Studies about LGBTQ students in special-mission institutions (for example, historically Black colleges and universities, religiously affiliated institutions, or women's colleges) make additional contributions to this literature (Hart & Lester, 2011; Killelea McEntarfer, 2011; Marine, 2011; Means & Jaeger, 2013; Mobley & Johnson, 2015; Patton, 2011; Wentz & Wessel, 2011). Taken as a whole in the context of widespread changes in public attitudes and public policies related to LGBTQ people, this enlarged body of research on LGBTQ students in higher education merits a sourcebook such as this one that synthesizes knowledge and posits connections to student affairs practice.

Notes About Terminology

The landscape of terminology related to social identity characteristics and social group memberships is fluid, changing, and contested. Over time, scholars and community activists have challenged some of the language customarily used to refer to people whose identities and group memberships have lower status, visibility, and power in society. In particular, *minority* as a term for those groups with less status, visibility, and power fails to reflect the systematic and structural oppression in society that results in some groups having higher status, visibility, and power than others. In certain contexts, it can also be factually inaccurate; not all groups who have less status, visibility, and power are necessarily fewer in number than those groups who do. The coming "majority-minority" racial and ethnic composition of the United States and of some colleges and universities is one example.

The lower status, visibility, and power of some groups compared to others are the result of a process of systematic and structural oppression. These social identities and social groups do not have less status, visibility,

New Directions for Student Services, no. 152, Winter 2015 © 2015 Wiley Periodicals, Inc.
Published online in Wiley Online Library (wileyonlinelibrary.com) • DOI: 10.1002/ss.20141

and power as a natural outcome of their differences. On the contrary, this outcome is a function of the myriad ways that social groups with valued ways of being in the world continue to accrue greater resources and visibility, maintain high status and power, and define what is normal, optimal, and neutral (Johnson, 2005). Therefore, in this volume, we follow the increasingly common practice of an interdisciplinary community of scholars (such as Benitez, 2010; Chase, Dowd, Pazich, & Bensimon, 2014; Gillborn, 2005; Godard, Mukjerjee, & Mukherjee, 2006; Patton, Harper, & Harris, 2015) to use the term *minoritized* as we discuss those whose sexuality and gender have been consigned to lower status, visibility, and power.

Although this language helps frame the larger group of students we are discussing in this volume, students with minoritized sexual and gender identities, the terminology to describe those within this larger umbrella is also dynamic and contested as T.J. Jourian illustrates in the first chapter. Simply put, there is no universally accepted set of terms for describing students from minoritized sexual orientation or gender identity groups. In naming this volume, we chose to use lesbian, gay, and bisexual for minoritized sexual identities; transgender for minoritized gender identities; and queer, which includes minoritized identities in either category. In part because of its relative ease as a search term in the United States and many other nations, we use the abbreviation LGBTQ in the text we composed. But there are a host of other terms and abbreviations circulating in the literature and in educational practice that we might have chosen instead, among them asexual, pansexual, trans∗, intersex, questioning, LGBT, LGBT+, LGBTQIA, and so forth.

In acknowledgment of the diversity of terminology in use in the field and in the literature, we opted to have chapter authors select their own terms and give a brief explanation. Some readers will use the entire volume and thus encounter different terms across chapters, whereas others will use one or a few chapters, perhaps without noticing these differences. We encourage readers to develop their own views on terminology, based in their own epistemologies and ideological commitments. We also encourage readers to be alert to changing terminology in the field and to respect the terms that individuals use to describe their identities, even as those terms change over time and situation.

Ecology of LGBTQ College Students

We have organized this sourcebook around an ecological understanding of LGBTQ college students in the contexts of their lives on and off campus. We believe that locating individuals in the context of their environments, and different elements of the environment in interaction with the individual and with one another, is an effective way to understand how best to serve LGBTQ students in the evolving sociopolitical milieu of LGBTQ issues in the 21st century. An ecological perspective also enables us to integrate

NEW DIRECTIONS FOR STUDENT SERVICES • DOI: 10.1002/ss

concepts that are in common across the many component groups that fall under the "LGBTQ" umbrella: lesbians, gay men, bisexuals, transgender and gender queer individuals, racial and ethnic communities, faith communities, and other identities that individual LGBTQ people may hold. Rather than have a chapter on each group, we address these topics holistically, from a discussion of the evolving nature of sexual orientation and gender identity (Chapter One), to identities and institutional contexts (Chapter Two), to two key campus environments (Curricular/Classroom in Chapter Three; Cocurricular/Campus life in Chapter Four) and assessment and research (Chapter Five). Each chapter addresses multiple and intersecting identities of LGBTQ students in a range of institutional types.

The main ecological perspective from which we draw is that of Urie Bronfenbrenner (1993; Bronfenbrenner & Morris, 2006), who proposed a model composed of four elements: Person, Process, Context, and Time (PPCT). Person involves demographics, experiences, and personal characteristics such as inclination to undertake increasingly complex tasks and propensity to engage with the environment. Developmental processes require increasingly complex interactions in the proximal environment, balanced with adequate buffers and supports, evoking the familiar challenge and support approach articulated by Nevitt Sanford (1962). These processes take place in the context of a student's life on and off campus. Renn and Arnold (2003) depicted a nested system of contexts spanning out from the microsystems in which a student has direct interaction, such as roommates, family, courses, lab groups, sports teams, workplace, and student clubs. Mesosystems are the next level out, in which students encounter interactions between and among microsystems, as when expectations from family contrast with or reinforce expectations of faculty, peers, coaches, and work supervisors. The exosystem represents a level in which the student is not present but that influences the student's development indirectly, for example, when faculty committees set curricula, policy makers define financial aid eligibility requirements, the vice president of student affairs approves gender-inclusive (also called gender-neutral) housing on campus, or parents experience workplace change that affects family income.

Finally, the macrosystem contains larger sociohistorical forces and culture that influence developmental possibilities; for LGBTQ students, these forces include public policy related to civil rights (participation in the military, marriage, workplace and educational nondiscrimination), the healthcare system (availability and affordability of gender-related medical services), and attitudes toward gender and sexual orientation minorities. In Bronfenbrenner's (1993) model, Time acts in both incremental ways and as a larger demarcation of sociocultural change. The PPCT approach to developmental ecology provides a useful frame for understanding the experiences and identities of LGBTQ college students. Personal characteristics interact with each level of the context to influence subsequent development and experiences.

We structured this sourcebook around the concepts of the PPCT model (Bronfenbrenner, 1993). The model takes into account multiple campus settings (microsystems) in which LGBTQ students live, learn, and develop. We purposefully include academic and cocurricular settings at the micro-, meso-, and exosystem levels. Institutional policy and faculty curriculum committees, for example, act primarily at the exosystem level to create changes in campus climate, classroom experiences, and available areas of study at the micro level. We urge readers to keep the totality of this ecosystem model—or some other person–environment model they may prefer—in mind when considering LGBTQ students in the contexts presented in the chapters. An ecological approach is evident particularly in Chapter Two, in which the authors present a new model of Minoritized Identities of Sexuality and Gender.

Competency-Based, Appreciative Approach

As important as the ecology model was to our conception of the sourcebook, taking a competency-based and appreciative approach to LGBTQ students was important to framing the content. We embrace the notion of a competency- or strengths-based approach, which assumes that LGBTQ students have resilience and resources they bring to bear as agents in constructing their college experiences and identities. Appreciative inquiry in higher education (see Cockell & McArthur-Blair, 2012) is a positive, coconstructive, potentially transformative approach to understanding phenomena in context. Cockell and McArthur-Blair (2012) quoted Marjorie Schiller describing appreciative inquiry as a "co-constructed practice informed by all those who work on creating the conditions for growth and change based upon seeking the positive core" (p. 2). Together, the focus on competence and appreciative inquiry form a positive, forward-looking foundation from which to understand the experiences, identities, and outcomes of LGBTQ students.

Appreciative inquiry is at its core an approach that works in contrast to deficit models, which once dominated policy, practice, and research related to LGBTQ students. Dilley (2002), Marine (2011), and others have demonstrated a history of college officials treating nonheterosexual students as deviant, diseased, or at minimum in need of counseling to cope with what was assumed to be an unfortunate lot in life. Even the turn toward campus climate studies (for example, Rankin, Weber, Blumenfeld, & Frazer, 2010) relies on demonstrating the hardships LGBTQ students face. To be clear, we believe that campus climate studies are critical elements of a comprehensive approach to understanding obstacles to educational equity, but they are not sufficient to describe the reality of the college experience of LGBTQ students. If 30% of lesbian, gay, and bisexual respondents to the 2010 National Campus Climate Study (Rankin et al., 2010) reported feeling intimidated or bullied, that means that 70% did not. And what is going on in the (we hope) vast majority of time that LGBTQ students spend on campus when they are not being harassed? Just as literature about successful students from racial and ethnic groups minoritized in U.S. higher education (see Harper, 2010, 2013; Patton, 2009; Pérez, 2014) uses a competency-based, antideficit lens to make visible the identities, experiences, and perceptions of underrepresented students, in this sourcebook we aim to present a synthesis of literature on LGBTQ students that starts from a place of success and resilience. Such a perspective is consonant with an ecological approach, in that personal characteristics and environmental buffers and supports provide positive counterforces to negative campus climate and discriminatory incidents. This appreciative, competency-based approach is evident throughout the sourcebook.

Multiple Identities and Intersections of Systems of Oppression

It is impossible to bracket sexual orientation and gender identities to consider them apart from the whole student. A trend in the literature since the early 2000s has been to study students' multiple identities (see Abes, Jones & McEwen, 2007; Jones & Abes, 2013; Jones & McEwen, 2000), placing various aspects of identity in constant coconstruction with one another within the context of personal development and the environment. A subset of LGBTQ college student literature addresses specific combinations of sexual orientation or gender identity with, for example, race or religion. Abes (2012) explored intersections of identity for a Catholic lesbian student. Patton (2011) described identity, disclosure, and environment for gay and bisexual men at an historically Black college. Hayes, Chun-Kennedy, Edens, and Locke (2011) found that sexual and ethnic minority students experienced more stress than students who were in only one of these two minorities. Means and Jaeger (2013) employed "quare theory," which is based on intersections of race, gender, class, and sexual orientation, to analyze the experiences of Black gay male students at historically Black colleges and universities. These examples point to the ways that scholars are investigating multiple identities and intersections of systems of oppression. Work of this type continues and is likely to be a fruitful line of inquiry for some time.

We recognize the value of these studies of specific combinations and increasingly sophisticated theoretical contributions to understanding multiple identities. Rather than present a chapter on LGBTQ students of color or LGBTQ students of particular religious faiths, we have integrated issues related to students' multiple identities into each chapter. This approach is consistent with our ecological frame, which defies parsing of identities and emphasizes the whole student interacting with and within various systems and levels of the environment. Our approach is also consistent with predominant thinking about multiple identities in contemporary higher education settings (see Jones & Abes, 2013). Intersections are a key feature of the discussion in Chapter One of the evolving nature of sexual orientation and gender identity, and they are key features in Chapter Five, which addresses research and assessment of diverse LGBTQ college students.

It is important to recognize that students experience intersections of systems of oppression. An upper-middle class, cisgender Latina lesbian is subject to forces of classism, genderism, sexism, racism, and heterosexism, though as a member of privileged groups (upper-middle class, cisgender) she may not recognize the effects of this privilege in her life. Her working class, transgender White asexual roommate may perceive classism, genderism, and heterosexism, but not racism. Higher education is a context in which these—and other—systems of oppression play out and, in some cases, reinforce power differences among groups. Moreover, membership in privileged social groups alters how individuals experience and navigate their membership in marginalized social groups. Likewise, experiences with marginality influence the construction of privileged identities.

This sourcebook focuses on identities, demographics, and institutional contexts in Chapter Two in order to portray the interactions among individuals and groups on campuses that exist within larger social structures of privilege and oppression. The authors include personal characteristics, such as ways of thinking and being (for example, in Myers-Briggs Type Indicator types), as well as institutional features such as size, control (public, private, denominational), and region. Macro features, such as immediate, repeated/recent, and historical time, create a context for the enactment of sociocultural influences on the experiences and identities of LGBTQ students.

Chapters Three and Four describe academic and cocurricular/campus life environments, respectively. These are the two main on-campus ecosystems in which students encounter peers, faculty, and professional staff. Students also encounter human-built aspects of campus life (for example, policies, organizations, media, architecture, and physical artifacts) that may be variably supportive of them as LGBTQ people (see Renn, Woodford, Nicolazzo, & Brazelton, 2014). Chapter authors consider students' multiple identities operating within intersections of systems of oppression, an ecological approach to understanding academic and student life.

International and Global Perspectives

As higher education becomes increasingly global, it is important to understand LGBTQ students within international contexts. What does it mean for an LGBTQ international student to come from a country with more repressive—or more progressive—laws than the United States? What happens when they return home after graduation? What is it like for an LGBTQ student to select a study-abroad experience in a world that spans from openly embracing sexual orientation and gender identity diversity to maintaining death sentences for homosexual activity? How can educators prepare them for such an experience? What happens to campus climate when domestic students (who may themselves come from states with different degrees of civil rights for LGBTQ people and families with a range of social, political, and religious viewpoints) and international students who, because of the way that their home nation treats LGBTQ people, have never had a chance to meet an openly LGBTQ person or discuss LGBTQ rights share a campus? Or an international student's first consciousness of a same-gender-loving or trans∗ identity happens while they are studying in the United States? These questions—and others like them—circulate throughout the topics we address in this sourcebook.

The sourcebook is U.S.-centric; that is, although we hope it will be useful to educators outside the United States, the literature on which it is based comes largely from studies of college students in the United States. We did, however, encourage chapter authors to include international issues and topics of globalization to the greatest extent possible. For example, Chapter One includes a discussion of how international students may understand and react to common terms related to gender identity and sexuality in the-United States, and Chapter Four includes international contexts outside the classroom.

Content of the Sourcebook

In Chapter One, T.J. Jourian discusses the continued evolution of terminology, constructs, and ideologies that inform the language used by those who are lesbian, gay, bisexual, and same-gender loving, who may identify as queer, as well as those who are members of trans∗ communities. Jourian describes the historical evolution and present status of these debates and resolutions as critical guideposts for what the future might hold for upcoming generations of college students. As part of this dialogue, Jourian includes research on multiple identities and the intersections of privilege and oppression within individuals in these LGBTQ communities.

In Chapter Two, Annemarie Vaccaro, E. I. Annie Russell, and Robert M. Koob situate their discussion in light of the paradox inherent in the coexistence of evolving fluidity of language with limitations created by limited, standardized bureaucratic categories used for institutional classifications (for example, sex or race). The authors discuss demographics of college students with minoritized identities of sexuality and gender (MIoSG) across institutional types in the United States. They offer a new ecological framework for understanding the intersections of sociopolitical systems, campus context, homeplace, self, meaning making processes, and time. Institutional/campus contexts, including uniqueness of type, history, mission, structure, policies, campus initiatives, and unstructured events/interactions are central aspects of this new model. They conclude by offering suggestions about how practitioners can utilize the model to create inclusive spaces in any institutional context.

Jodi Linley and David Nguyen, in Chapter Three, consider the impact of climate on students, faculty, and staff. Through an examination of the representation and visibility of LGBTQ faculty and staff, and scholarly topics related to LGBTQ lives, they discuss how students experience and display identities in academic contexts. They emphasize the ways in which LGBTQ students use strategies of resilience, and describe best practices and competencies educators need to help students navigate and succeed.

Debbie Bazarsky, Leslie Morrow, and Gabriel Javier present in Chapter Four the corollary to the preceding chapter. Their focus is on cocurricular and campus life environmental influences on LGBTQ students. They explore representation and visibility of LGBTQ models and mentors across student affairs and auxiliary services, as well as opportunities and challenges for LGBTQ-inclusive campus climates across campus areas (e.g., residence halls, off-campus residences, neighborhood engagement, health and wellness centers, recreation and athletics, career services). They also discuss issues of leadership, activism, advocacy, involvement, and engagement. A critical question this chapter addresses relates to whether support services for LGBTQ students exist and how they integrate with other identity-based resources and support.

Sue Rankin and Jason Garvey discuss topics related to assessment and research with LGBTQ campus communities, connections to student success research, and the role of institutional research units in Chapter Five. Rankin and Garvey address a number of issues, including the need or desire to be able to count LGBTQ students in higher education; practices and policies related to asking for sexual orientation and gender identity on admission applications; the imperative not to conflate sexual orientation and gender identity; and the role of critical quantitative research and nonpositivist methodologies in research and assessment. The authors also revisit some of the language issues addressed earlier in the monograph (in most chapters but especially Chapter One) by considering what it means to ask questions about sexual orientation and gender identity and how to ask such questions. Rankin and Garvey consider the need intentionally to interrogate multiple identities and intersecting privileges and marginalities wherein LGBTQ students may experience prejudice and bias in communities presumed otherwise "safe" for them to express their identities.

Finally, we as editors join again in the final chapter to consider the key ideas and points raised throughout the monograph and offer recommendations for research, policy, and practice. We locate this volume in the intellectual trajectory and history of educational practice vis-à-vis LGBTQ students. We provide final commentary on the state of research in the field, and make recommendations for future directions for research, theory, and educational practice.

Dafina-Lazarus Stewart
Kristen A. Renn
G. Blue Brazelton
Editors

References

Abes. E. S. (2012). Constructivist and intersectional interpretations of a lesbian college student's multiple social identities. *Journal of Higher Education, 83*(2), 186-216.

Abes, E. S., Jones, S. R., & McEwen, M. K. (2007). Reconceptualizing the model of multiple dimensions of identity: The role of meaning-making capacity in the construction of multiple identities. *Journal of College Student Development, 48*(1), 1-22.

Benitez, M. (2010). Resituating culture centers within a social justice framework: Is there room for examining whiteness? In L. Patton (Ed.), *Culture centers in higher education: Perspectives on identity, theory, and practice* (pp. 119-136). Sterling, VA: Stylus.

Bronfenbrenner, U. (1993). The ecology of cognitive development: Research models and fugitive findings. In R. H. Wozniak & K. W. Fischer (Eds.), *Development in context: Acting and thinking in specific environments* (pp. 3-44). Hillsdale, NJ: Erlbaum.

Bronfenbrenner, U., & Morris, P. A. (2006). The bioecological model of human development. In W. Damon & R. M. Lerner (Eds.), *Handbook of child psychology* (6th ed., pp. 793-828). Hoboken, NJ: Wiley.

Chase, M. M., Dowd, A. C., Pazich, L. B., & Bensimon, E. M. (2014). Transfer equity for "minoritized" students: A critical policy analysis of seven states. *Educational Policy, 28*(5), 669-717.

Cockell, J., & McArthur-Blair, J. (2012). *Appreciative inquiry in higher education: A transformative force*. San Francisco: John Wiley & Sons.

Dilley, P. (2002). *Queer man on campus: A history of non-heterosexual college men, 1945-2000*. New York: Routledge.

Gillborn, D. (2005). Education policy as an act of White supremacy: Whiteness, critical race theory and education reform. *Journal of Education Policy, 20*(4), 485-505.

Godard, B. J., Mukjerjee, A. P., & Mukherjee, A. (2006). Translating minoritized cultures: Issues of caste, class and gender. *Postcolonial Text, 2*(3), 1-23.

Harper, S. R. (2010). An anti-deficit achievement framework for research on students of color in STEM. In S. R. Harper & C. B. Newman (Eds.), *New Directions for Institutional Research: No. 148. Students of color in STEM* (pp. 63-74). San Francisco, CA: Jossey-Bass.

Harper, S. R. (2013). Am I my brother's teacher? Black undergraduates, racial socialization, and peer pedagogies in predominantly white postsecondary contexts. *Review of Research in Education, 37*(1), 183-211.

Hart, J., & Lester, J. (2011). Starring students: Gender performance at a women's college. *NASPA Journal about Women in Higher Education, 4*(2), 193-217.

Hayes, J. A., Chun-Kennedy, C., Edens, A., & Locke, B. D. (2011). Do double minority students face double jeopardy? Testing minority stress theory. *Journal of College Counseling, 14*(2), 117-126.

Johnson, A. G. (2005). *Privilege, power, and difference* (2nd ed.). New York, NY: McGraw-Hill.

Jones, S. R., & Abes, E. S. (2013). *Identity development of college students: Advancing frameworks for multiple dimensions of identity*. San Francisco: John Wiley & Sons.

Jones, S. R., & McEwen, M. K. (2000). A conceptual model of multiple dimensions of identity. *Journal of College Student Development, 41*(4), 405-414.

Killelea McEntarfer, H. (2011). "Not going away": Approaches used by students, faculty, and staff members to create gay–straight alliances at three religiously affiliated universities. *Journal of LGBT Youth, 8*(4), 309-331.

Marine, S. (2011). Special issue: Stonewall's legacy—Bisexual, gay, lesbian, and transgender students in higher education. [*ASHE Higher Education Report, 37*(4)]. San Francisco, CA: Jossey-Bass.

Means, D. R., & Jaeger, A. J. (2013). Black in the rainbow: "Quaring" the black gay male student experience at historically Black universities. *Journal of African American Males in Education, 4*(2), 124-140.

Mobley, S. D., Jr., & Johnson, J. M. (2015). The role of HBCUs in addressing the unique needs of LGBT students. In. R. T. Palmer, C. R. Shorette, & M. Gasman (Eds.), *New Directions for Higher Education: No 170. Exploring diversity at historically black colleges and universities: Implications for policy and practice* (pp. 79–89). San Francisco, CA: Jossey-Bass.

Patton, L. D. (2009). My sister's keeper: A qualitative examination of mentoring experiences among African American women in graduate and professional schools. *Journal of Higher Education, 80*(5), 510–537.

Patton, L. D. (2011). Perspectives on identity, disclosure, and the campus environment among African American gay and bisexual men at one historically black college. *Journal of College Student Development, 52*(1), 77–100.

Patton, L. D., Harper, S. R., & Harris, J. (2015). Using critical race theory to (re)interpret widely studied topics related to U.S. higher education. In A. M. Martinez-Alemán, B. Pusser, & E. M. Bensimon (Eds.), *Critical approaches to the study of higher education: A practical introduction* (pp. 193–219). Baltimore, MD: Johns Hopkins University.

Pérez, D. (2014). Exploring the nexus between community cultural wealth and the academic and social experiences of Latino male achievers at two predominantly White research universities. *International Journal of Qualitative Studies in Education, 27*(6), 747–767.

Rankin, S., Weber, G., Blumenfeld, W., & Frazer, S. (2010). *2010 state of higher education for lesbian, gay, bisexual & transgender people.* Charlotte, NC: Campus Pride.

Renn, K. A., & Arnold, K. D. (2003). Reconceptualizing research on peer culture. *Journal of Higher Education, 74,* 261–291.

Renn, K. A., Woodford, M., R., Nicolazzo, Z., & Brazelton, G. B. (2014, April). *The role of personal resilience and environmental buffers in LGBTQ college student success.* Paper presented at the annual meeting of the American Educational Research Association, Philadelphia, PA.

Sanford, N. (1962). The developmental status of the entering freshman. In N. Sanford (Ed.), *The American college student* (pp. 253–282). Hoboken, NJ: Wiley.

Sanlo, R. L. (Ed.). (2005). *New Directions for Student Services: No. 111. Gender identity and sexual orientation: Research, policy, and personal perspectives.* San Francisco, CA: Jossey-Bass.

Wentz, J., & Wessel, R. D. (2011). The intersection of gay and Christian identities on Christian college campuses. *Journal of College and Character, 12*(2), 1–6.

DAFINA-LAZARUS STEWART *is associate professor of higher education and student affairs at Bowling Green State University.*

KRISTEN A. RENN *is professor of higher, adult, and lifelong education at Michigan State University.*

G. BLUE BRAZELTON *is assistant professor of higher education and student affairs at Northern Michigan University.*

NEW DIRECTIONS FOR STUDENT SERVICES • DOI: 10.1002/ss

1

This chapter discusses the historical and evolving terminology, constructs, and ideologies that inform the language used by those who are lesbian, gay, bisexual, and same-gender loving, who may identify as queer, as well as those who are members of trans* communities from multiple and intersectional perspectives.

Evolving Nature of Sexual Orientation and Gender Identity

T.J. Jourian

In 2013 Pink Therapy, a U.K.-based counseling organization, proposed replacing the LGBT (lesbian, gay, bisexual, and transgender) acronym with GSD (gender and sexual diversities; Sansalone, 2013). The group argued that LGBT and variations of it such as LGBTQQIA (to include queer, questioning, intersex, and asexual people) cannot include the multitude of identities with which people identify. In the United States, the University of Michigan's Spectrum Center has been renamed numerous times over its almost 35 years of existence (Burris, n.d.). These are but two examples of how language used to describe sexuality and gender continues to shift and in turn can influence and/or communicate the work student affairs professionals do with college students.

This chapter provides an overview of some of the ways sexual orientation and gender identity have been and are discussed in the United States, with particular attention paid to language in higher education institutions. Beginning with an historical overview, the chapter moves into current understandings of sex, gender, and sexual orientation, as contextualized within systems of oppression and privilege, and ends with the queering and constantly evolving nature of terminology relevant to sexual orientation and gender identity. For consistency the acronym LGBTQ is used throughout this chapter, unless referencing particular subpopulations, using official organizational names, or citing specific literature. This chapter is not meant to be, nor can or should it be, an exhaustive collection of definitions and terminology, but rather it serves as an opening to help situate the complex intricacies, intentions, and limitations that may inform how some students identify.

New Directions for Student Services, no. 152, Winter 2015 © 2015 Wiley Periodicals, Inc.
Published online in Wiley Online Library (wileyonlinelibrary.com) • DOI: 10.1002/ss.20142

11

Historical Overview

The behaviors and expressions that many in the United States associate with LGBTQ identities have long existed in many preindustrial societies worldwide. However, the terms used by higher education and student affairs professionals today to describe them are recent "inventions." Here "invention" does not mean "inventing" nonheterosexual desires or gender nonconformity but rather the act of naming and categorizing those realities. These terms began to emerge in Europe in the 19th century (Foucault, 1978). The "invention" of *homosexuality* in the United States was specifically tied to race and racism with the increasing and often simultaneous policing and legislating of both racial and sexual boundaries and the emergence of their accompanied bifurcations, in other words, "Black" or "White," "heterosexual" or "homosexual" (Ferguson, 2004; Somerville, 2000). *Transgender* came into common parlance through the U.S. medical establishment in the 1960s, gaining widespread use in the early 1990s (Rawson & Williams, 2014).

LGBTQ people existed well before these times. In precolonial North America, for example, gender-variant individuals existed in hundreds of indigenous populations, including the *winkte* of the Lakota, the *nadleehe* of the Navajo, and the *lhamana* of the Zuni, to name a few (Gilley, 2006; Rifkin, 2011). Today, Two-Spirit is used to collectively express North American indigenous gender-variant people's identities. Two-Spirit is often uncritically equated with LGBTQ identities, meaning it is "translated" through a colonial and Euro-Western lens rather than understood within its own historicity and cultural context (Cameron, 2005). It is thus at the very least incomplete to responsibly and ethically review the historical evolution of these terms without a recognition that colonialism and racism have shaped that evolution and how in turn communities of color have resisted the erasure of their ways of knowing through resurrections and recreations of language.

Terms associated with LGBTQ identities that are used today in the United States did not come to be until the early to mid-20th century and thus also do not appear when specifically looking within higher education. Same-sex eroticism and partnerships prior to that time were referenced as "romantic friendships" and "crushes" (rather tritely and usually in the case of students at women's colleges; MacKay, 1993) or as abhorrent and a problem (Dilley, 2002). Terms used on college campuses also reflected language used by those who had access to higher education. For example, "butch" and "femme" have been widely used identifiers among working-class lesbian women since the 1950s (Nestle, 1981), but they do not surface in higher education discourse as access to college was almost exclusively limited to those with financial means.

LGBTQ people progressively entered into everyday people's consciousness locally and nationally largely due to protests and movements such as

NEW DIRECTIONS FOR STUDENT SERVICES • DOI: 10.1002/ss

the Harlem Renaissance of the 1920s through the 1940s, the Civil Rights Movement of the 1950s and 1960s, the 1966 Compton Cafeteria riot, the 1969 Stonewall riots, and AIDS activism of the 1980s and 1990s (D'Emilio, 2010; Schwartz, 2003; Stryker, 2008; Wolf, 2009). Language used to describe nonheterosexual desires and gender nonconformity in higher education often mirrored and was influenced by the social movements of the time. The founding of groups such as the Mattachine Society and the Daughters of Bilitis in the 1950s marked the beginnings of the homophile movement, mirrored in the formation of the first campus-based organizations known as Student Homophile Leagues (SHLs) in the mid-1960s (Marine, 2011). As "homophile" began to be replaced by the use of the word "gay," such as with the Gay Liberation Front, a similar linguistic shift occurred on college campuses. For example, the SHL at Columbia changed its name to Gay People at Columbia-Barnard. Concurrently, critiques were offered of the word "gay" being used as a blanket term to reference a diversity of nonheterosexual and gender-nonconforming identities. These criticisms often came from White women, people of color across genders, and trans* people of various races and ethnicities, who understood "gay" to exclude anyone other than cisgender White men with same-sex desires (Wolf, 2009). On campuses these criticisms are reflected through renaming some student organizations to communicate broader inclusion, and the creations of student organizations focused on particular subsets of the population as are discussed later in this chapter.

Social movements not only played a role in the formation and naming of student organizations and centers on college campuses but also in the development of theoretical literature informing student affairs practice. Research examining sexual orientation development in the 1970s resulted in Homosexual or Gay Identity Development models (for example, Cass, 1979; Troiden, 1979). Subsequent models are referred to as Lesbian, Gay, Bisexual, and/or Transgender Identity Development. How the models were named was often also a marker of which subpopulations were included in the research and whether the model focused on sexual orientation and/or gender identity (for example, Bilodeau, 2005; D'Augelli, 1994; Fox, 1995). Mirroring the aforementioned critiques of the word "gay" and resistance to the erasure of culturally distinct terminology, researchers also named people and identities at varying intersections of sexuality, gender, and race (for example, Manalansan, 1993; Parks, 2001; Vidal-Ortiz, 2011; Wilson, 1996). Some of these terms are explored in the next section.

Foundational Concepts: Sex, Gender, and Sexual Orientation

Higher education scholarship and practice within the last decade have used a model that distinguishes between four components of sexual identity (Lev, 2004): sex, gender identity, gender expression, and sexual orientation. The four components are interrelated but separate. Sex, more accurately described as sex assigned at birth, refers to "the physiological makeup of a human being" (Lev, 2004, p. 80), meaning how one's genes, hormones, biochemistry, and internal and external anatomy combine to affect the physical body. The most common sex assignments are male and female, despite a wide range of variation in sexual development in human beings that do not neatly fit into either (Fausto-Sterling, 2000). *Intersex* or people with *Differences of Sexual Development* (DSD; Diamond, 2009) are used to describe those who physiologically deviate from the sex binary. Intersex people have a variety of gender identities, just like males and females.

Gender, which is often conflated and used interchangeably with sex, refers to the sociohistorically and culturally constructed roles and attributes given to people, often based on their assigned sex. A person's own self-conception of gender is referred to as one's gender identity, whereas the performance and enactment of gender is referred to as one's gender expression. Words that describe gender identity include woman, man, genderqueer, transgender, agender, and endless others, whereas terms such as masculine, androgynous, feminine, and many more describe gender expression. Some descriptors such as butch, femme, transfeminine, and masculine-of-center may refer to one's gender identity or gender expression or a melding of both. Within social institutions and cultures that reify essentialist and binary understandings of gender, such as U.S. higher education institutions, those assigned as males at birth are expected to be masculine men and those assigned females at birth are expected to be feminine women (Bilodeau, 2009). Fluidity and alternatives are rarely acknowledged or affirmed.

Finally, sexual orientation encompasses one's romantic, sexual, and/or emotional attractions to others. The labels people use to describe their sexual orientation, also known as sexual identity or sexuality, are vast. They include heterosexual, gay, lesbian, bisexual, queer, asexual, and same-gender loving (SGL), to name a few. SGL emerged in the early 1990s as a culturally affirming Afrocentric alternative to the terms gay and lesbian and is used primarily within the African American community. Sexuality also involves sexual behaviors, which are the actions in which one engages with oneself or others. Understanding of this aspect has been informed by the Kinsey scale (Kinsey, Pomeroy, & Martin, 1948; Kinsey, Pomeroy, Martin, & Gebhard, 1953) and the Klein (1978) sexual orientation grid, describing sexual orientation as a nonbinary construct. These models demonstrate that people cannot all be identified as either homosexual or heterosexual exclusively. Kinsey uses a scale from 0 (exclusively heterosexual) to 6 (exclusively homosexual), with "x" used to describe asexuality. Klein's grid rates seven different variables (sexual attraction, sexual behavior, sexual fantasies, emotional preference, social preference, heterosexual/homosexual lifestyle, and self-identification) using a 1 (exclusively heterosexual) to 7 (exclusively homosexual) scale, across three different points in time: the past, the present, and the ideal. Sell (1996) measures heterosexuality and homosexuality independently from each other and not on a continuum as

Lev, Klein, and Kinsey do. Additionally, Sell distinguishes sexual attraction, sexual behavior, and sexual identity from each other, indicating that the type of person to whom one might be attracted and one's identity or behavior may not match. For example, a woman who is sexually attracted to other women and may even engage in sexual activity with women may identify as heterosexual. This may be the case if the woman in question does not wish to or cannot be open about her sexual attractions, or because she does not experience emotional attraction to other women and thus identifies as heterosexual due to her romantic inclination toward men. Another woman engaging in similar dynamics might identify herself as bisexual.

Viewing the four categories of sex, gender identity, gender expression, and sexual orientation as four interactive, fluid, and nonbinary continua allows us to discuss gender and sexuality in complex and nuanced ways that provide room for agency and self-determination. Although the distinctions between the four are useful in some ways—such as to demonstrate that a transgender woman can be a lesbian, just as much as she can be heterosexual, or any other sexual orientation—these distinctions are not necessarily cross-culturally applicable. Extremely rigid distinctions between these components often leave out communities and people that conceptualize a more integrated relationship between gender and sexuality, often in ways different from White and Western understandings of them. This includes māhū people in traditional Hawaiian culture, the fa'afafine in Samoan culture, or studs in the United States. Thus, it is important not simply to impose Eurocentric language (for example, by saying fa'afafine is Samoan for transgender) but to learn how different cultures conceptualize gender and sexuality through their histories and traditions as well as about the role of colonialism and racism in marginalizing sexual and gender diversity in communities of color. For an educational resource, see the recently released documentary, *Kumu Hina* (Hamer, Wilson, & Florez, 2014).

Situating Students Within Systems of Oppression

Often when discussing LGBTQ students and matters concerning sexual orientation and gender identity, it is important to identify and contextualize the systems of oppression that affect students' experiences on and off campuses, as well as their access to and development of identities and discourse. The systems most identifiable as affecting these student populations are *heterosexism*, *monosexism*, and *genderism/cissexism*. These systems interact with and are informed by others such as *sexism*, *racism*, *ethnocentrism*, *classism*, *ableism*, and *xenophobia*, as exemplified previously when examining historical and contemporary development of terminology and concepts. Students' multiple identities converge with each other and are informed by varying contexts and levels of salience of each of their identities to their core sense of selves. For example, let us minimally compare a lesbian cisgender woman of color who is an engineering major at a large institution with a White lesbian trans∗ woman who is an elementary education major at a small liberal arts college. Although both identify as lesbians, their other identities, the types of environments with which they interact most, and how salient their racial, sexual, and gender identities are to them will likely have an impact on the ways they experience and understand heterosexism.

Heterosexism is based on the presumption that everyone is heterosexual. This presumption leads to a systemic institutionalization of attitudes and biases that privileges those who identify as heterosexual and/or are in heterosexual relationships. It posits heterosexual identities and relationships as the norm and thus superior to nonheterosexual ones. Based on the gender binary discussed previously, heterosexism relies on the notion that maleness/masculinity/men are oppositional, distinguishable from, and complementary to femaleness/femininity/women. As an example, the argument that gender-neutral housing leads to couples living together in the residence halls is based on the assumption that all students are heterosexual and thus the word "couple" implies only a man and woman pairing. *Homophobia* is a form of heterosexism that describes fear and/or hatred of nonheterosexual people and actions, language, or behavior that stem from that fear/hatred, such as the tearing down of flyers promoting a gay-identified speaker on campus.

Monosexism is based on the presumption that everyone is attracted to only one other sex or gender, meaning that one is either exclusively heterosexual or exclusively gay/lesbian. This presumption can show up, for example, when a male-identified student who had previously been in a relationship with another man starts dating a woman and is confronted by questions like, "So, are you straight now?" *Biphobia*, as a form of monosexism, is an aversion to bisexual and other non-monosexual people, such as pansexual or omnisexual, and is often based on negative stereotypes and invisibility/erasure of bisexuality (Eliason, 2000). These stereotypes include that bisexual people are indecisive and promiscuous or that bisexuality is just a phase or trendy.

Genderism or *cissexism* is rooted in the belief that there are only two genders and that gender is based on one's sex assignment at birth (Bilodeau, 2009). Genderism is institutionalized in higher education as a forced labeling process that sorts everyone into either "male" or "female," assigning privilege to those who conform to binary gender systems and punishing those who do not. Through genderism, trans∗ and gender-nonconforming identities are isolated, invisible, and thus not accessible. An example of genderism or cissexism that is common on college campuses is the lack of willingness or process to alter gender and sex designations in students' records or tying that process to surgical interventions, which are expensive, difficult to access, and may not be desired. *Transphobia*, as a form of genderism/cissexism, is a range of negative attitudes toward and devaluing and discriminatory treatment of trans∗ people. *Transmisogyny* describes how sexism and cissexism intersect to specifically oppress trans∗women (Serano, 2007), such as through their exclusion from many women's colleges.

Dyadism is the belief that there are only two "natural" and "biological" sexes, male and female. Dyadism is at the root of the widespread practice of nonconsensual genital surgery to which intersex infants are subjected when their external anatomy does not fit a prescribed standard of normalcy (for example, by having a large clitoris or a micro-penis). This is often followed by hormone therapy at adolescence, a practice that is referred to as concealment-centered model of care. *Interphobia* is prejudice, fear, and hatred toward intersex people and the behaviors that stem from it, such as using the pronoun "it" to describe people who identify as intersex.

LGBTQ students can also internalize these isms and phobias and hold oppressive views toward other LGBTQ people or themselves. This can be aimed at identities similar to their own (for example, a gay man holding negative attitudes toward other gay men who are "too gay" or "too feminine") or different (such as a lesbian woman believing that trans men are traitors). As these systems also intersect with other systems of oppression, social hierarchies and divisions are constructed among LGBTQ students, creating a compounding effect for people with multiple marginalized identities, such as LGBTQ people who are immigrants, disabled, and/or people of color. For example, a genderqueer deaf student might not be able to attend a confidential "coming out" support group, if ze (an example of a gender-neutral pronoun) cannot locate a queer-identified American Sign Language interpreter in the area to bring to an LGBTQ-only space. Other common examples include holding an LGBTQ 101 session for international students that assumes international students do not know about or value LGBTQ people, not considering physical accessibility when planning for LGBTQ-themed/friendly housing, or holding discussions on LGBTQ faith only from a Christian perspective.

Queering Terminology

As language evolves, terms describing sexuality and gender come and go, their meanings changing over time, in different contexts, and for different people. For example, it is rare today that an individual in the United States would self-identify as "homosexual," and its use is often seen as communicating disapproval or ignorance. A word used more widely in the United States today, and which confounds many, is the word "queer." Queer defies boundaries and does not have a clear singular definition. It is also not necessarily just about sexuality or gender, although it is predominantly used in that manner. "Queer is by definition whatever is at odds with the normal, the legitimate, the dominant . . . It is an identity without an essence" (Halperin, 1997, p. 62). Here I provide an overview of some of the ways the term is used and its different meanings.

Within academia, queer comes from queer theory or queer studies. Developed within poststructural critical theory in the early 1990s, queer theory questions the assumed normativity and stability of identities, structures, and discourse, such as dichotomous nature versus nurture debates. In and outside of academia, queer can convey a politic critical of mainstream LGBTQ approaches and priorities. Many queer activists and organizations such as Against Equality view the focus on marriage, participation in the military, and hate crimes legislation as assimilationist rather than liberatory, empowering structures that disproportionately oppress queer people of color, immigrants, and working-class people.

At an individual level, queer allows people to identify beyond gender and/or sexual binaries and name the fluidity and blurriness with which they experience those identities. For example, a student who views themselves in any way other than exclusively as a man or a woman may identify as genderqueer and may adopt gender-neutral pronouns such as "ze" (pronounced zee), "hir" (pronounced here), or the singular "they." Someone who finds themselves attracted to different genders or wishes to communicate an openness to that possibility may identify as queer, finding terms such as lesbian, gay, heterosexual, or even bisexual to be too confining. This does not imply that all bisexual people, for example, in turn define bisexuality in the same way but that the term does not work for the aforementioned student.

Adopting the term may also signal attempts to reclaim power from its use as a derogatory term. This does not mean that it can no longer be used as an insult, and in fact it still is. Queer has multiple meanings and interpretations, with some in the LGBT(Q) community not having an appreciation for the word. This can be due to generational, regional, and/or cultural reasons. Younger generations tend to be more comfortable with its use than older generations who have predominantly experienced it used negatively. The use of queer may be more contentious in the South than other parts of the United States. As a former program coordinator for a campus LGBTQI office in Tennessee, I found that the inclusion of Queer in the office's name puzzled and even angered people so much that explaining its many meanings was something I had to do at almost every tabling and training event. I did not experience this quite to that extent working at campuses in other regions of the country. Some people of color also perceive queer to be yet another White-centric term, with its connections to academia and lack of historic presence in communities of color. Other people of color do prefer queer as a descriptor or the intersectional terms QPOC (Queer People/Person of Color, pronounced Q-Pock) or QTPOC (Queer and Trans* People/Person of Color, pronounced Cutie-Pock) instead of LGBT people of color for many of the reasons already discussed in this section.

When naming gender and sexuality, agency and self-determination are crucial aspects of one's ability to describe one's own identity. Terms ought not to be imposed on individuals based solely on our own limited knowledge or our own interpretations of others' behaviors and expressions. In fact, discovering and even creating language for oneself can be an empowering experience for students, when they are affirmed in their process and afforded room to try different words without judgment ("I don't think that's a real identity, you shouldn't use it if you want people to understand you"), expectations ("You're queer, why are you wearing a suit and tie; that's so heteronormative"), or conditions ("You can't be queer and only like other women"). For student affairs professionals, using language (including pronouns) that an individual student identifies with in a given context at a given time is an important part of creating affirming, respectful, and safe spaces on campus.

Evolving Conversations and Complexities

In this section I focus on some current (and for some not-so-current) discussions and shifts in terminology. The intention is to provide additional examples at individual, communal, institutional, and societal levels of continued evolutions of language and in no part does it seek to be a comprehensive list. This would be both impossible and undesirable as the gender and sexual diversity within our communities cannot be fully captured in such a concise way. Additionally, the evolving and contextual natures of language require flexibility and a commitment to openness on our parts as educators and practitioners to new and sometimes challenging conversations and terminology.

Much of this evolution has to do with individuals and communities rejecting binary thinking. For some, this rejection directly relates to their own identities, prompting the search for and creation of language that better describes their identities more accurately. Non-monosexual identities are a clear example of rejecting a gay/lesbian or heterosexual binary. Individual people rarely self-identify as non-monosexual, rather using terms such as bisexual, pansexual, omnisexual, ambisexual, polysexual, and others. These labels help individuals express varying relationships to how gender factors into their own sexuality. Others seeking to communicate an openness in their monosexual identities might use terms such as heteroflexible (meaning primarily heterosexual, but open to the possibility of same-sex attraction) or homoflexible (the converse of heteroflexible).

In addition to sexuality, different terms used to describe one's gender identity may also communicate a nonbinary experience. Some of these terms include genderqueer, agender, bigender, gender nonconforming, intergender, gender fluid, neutrois, pangender, and many others. The asterisk at the end of the prefix trans is used to signal broad inclusivity of multiple gender identities beyond just trans men (also referred to as female-to-male or transgender men) or trans women (also referred to as male-to-female or transgender women), such as nonbinary individuals, as well as crossdressers and even gender performers like drag kings and

NEW DIRECTIONS FOR STUDENT SERVICES • DOI: 10.1002/ss

queens (Tompkins, 2014). This does not mean that all trans* people identify outside of the gender binary. In fact many individuals, some of whom may not use any trans*-related descriptors and prefer to be described simply as women or men, see themselves as very much aligned with one gender at all times. Some crossdressers and many gender performers also do not see themselves as part of the trans* community.

Terms are usually created to describe those perceived to be outside the norm, thus deciding who is considered normal and who is not. To resist this, trans* activist discourses in the 1990s began to use the term *cisgender* to describe those whose sex assignment at birth and gender identity aligned with each other in socially prescribed ways (Aultman, 2014). Cisgender is meant to replace terms such as normatively gendered or biologically gendered that by extension position trans* people as not normal or biological. The prefix *cis-* in Latin means "on the same side as," whereas the prefix *trans-* translates to "on the other side of," "beyond," or "across." By using "cis man" or "cis woman" instead of just "man" or "woman" when only discussing cisgender individuals resists the idea that a trans* person is not a man or a woman.

Terminology may also be created to identify gaps and commonalities within and across groups, both to form community and to enact social change. The coining of the term *masculine of center* (MoC) to describe "lesbian/queer womyn and gender-nonconforming/trans people who tilt towards the masculine side of the gender spectrum" (as cited in Bailey, 2014) allows individuals across genders and sexualities to build community with each other, as well as come together to form healthy masculinities. Relatedly, the term *brown boi* is used to describe MoC individuals, who are people of color. The Brown Boi Project (n.d.) is an organization that harnesses the leadership of brown bois toward intersectional gender justice.

Brown boi is one of many terms individuals and communities use to describe their identities intersectionally and not merely as additive. Earlier QPOC and QTPOC were introduced along with their pronunciations. The way the words are said is important as they phonetically communicate a merged racial, sexual, and gender identification that sounds different than saying LGBTQ people of color. Other intersectional terms, some of which may be appropriately used only as in-group terminology (meaning, by those who identify with these terms), include *gaysian* (merging gay and Asian) and *SDQ* (sick and disabled queers). Intersectional language may communicate one's resistance to having to pick between identities and express a more holistic self-conception and set of experiences. The growing number of QPOC/QTPOC student organizations and conferences around the country signals a need for spaces and movements that honor students' lives at the intersections of their many identities.

On college campuses, departments that serve students across diverse sexual and gender identities continue to contend with what to call themselves in order to best capture both this evolving terminology and ultimately whom they serve. In addition to the more ubiquitous LGBT or LGBTQ (with the letters in different orders at times), the current discussions on the inclusion or exclusion of two additional letters, I and A, reflect broader conversations on whether intersex and asexual people are part of the LGBTQ community. Intersex and asexual people themselves have diverse perspectives and experiences and thus do not hold a consensus on their positionalities. Some see themselves as part of the queer community, and others do not. As discussed previously, intersex people can hold a variety of gender identities, as well as may themselves identify as something other than heterosexual. Media representations of intersex people are extremely limited even today, with the MTV series *Faking It* (Nugiel, Goldman, Covington, Williams, & Leder, 2014) making history in 2014 by introducing the first main intersex character on a TV show.

Asexuality is often confused for abstinence, which describes a choice in behavior rather than a sexual orientation. People who practice abstinence do experience sexual attractions but have made the decision to not act on them for a period of time. Asexual is both an identity for people who do not experience sexual attraction to anyone and an umbrella term. Some asexual people do engage in purely romantic relationships and may find enjoyment in nonsexual physical activities such as cuddling. Various terms exist to describe asexual people's romantic inclinations, such as aromantic (do not experience romantic attractions), heteroromantic (romantically inclined toward people of a different sex/gender), homoromantic, biromantic, panromantic, and so on. Additionally, some may experience nonconsistent or occasional romantic and/or sexual attractions and may use terms such as gray-A (gray asexual), demiromantic, demisexual, and so on. These terms in turn communicate varying relationships with sexuality and romanticism. For example, demisexual people experience sexual attraction only when a stable emotional connection has been established. In a society where the existence of sexuality is a given, with phrases like "everyone has sex" seeming innocuous, asexual people may indeed feel queer themselves, meaning different from the given norm.

Students are often among the first to respond to changing terminology either by adopting them themselves when finding words to better describe who they are or by advocating for organizational name changes. Often less constrained by bureaucratic processes and institutional resistance that mire departmental-level changes, student organizations can quickly adapt to ensure inclusion and comfort. An example is when students at Vanderbilt University's Lambda GSA altered the acronym in their name to stand for Gender and Sexuality Alliance instead of Gay and Straight Alliance.

Names, labels, and language communicate a great deal about our knowledge, assumptions, intentions, and interpretations of particular topics and experiences. Practitioners and scholars have an ethical responsibility to cultivate an openness within themselves and campus-wide to shifting and contextually based terminology and to adopt practices that promote individual and community meaning making. This may merely be one part of creating equitable and inclusive campus communities for all students, but it is a crucial aspect.

References

Aultman, B. (2014). Cisgender. *Transgender Studies Quarterly*, 1(1–2), 61–63.

Bailey, V. (2014). Brown bois. *Transgender Studies Quarterly*, 1(1–2), 45–47.

Bilodeau, B. (2005). Beyond the gender binary: A case study of transgender college student development at a Midwestern university. *Journal of Gay and Lesbian Issues in Education*, 3(1), 29–44.

Bilodeau, B. L. (2009). *Genderism: Transgender students, binary systems and higher education*. Germany: VDM Verlag.

Brown Boi Project. (n.d.) [Website]. Retrieved from http://www.brownboiproject.org.

Burris, N. (n.d.). Our history. *Spectrum Center.* Retrieved from http://spectrumcenter.umich.edu/article/58.

Cameron, M. (2005). Two-spirited aboriginal people: Continuing cultural appropriation by non-aboriginal society. *Canadian Woman Studies*, 24(2), 123–127.

Cass, V. C. (1979). Homosexual identity formation: A theoretical model. *Journal of Homosexuality*, 4, 219–235.

D'Augelli, A. R. (1994). Identity development and sexual orientation: Toward a model of lesbian, gay, and bisexual development. In E. J. Trickett, R. J. Watts, & D. Birman (Eds.), *Human diversity: Perspectives of people in context* (pp. 312–333). San Francisco: Jossey-Bass.

D'Emilio, J. (2010). *Lost prophet: The life and times of Bayard Rustin*. New York: Simon & Schuster.

Diamond, M. (2009). Human intersexuality: Difference or disorder? *Sexual Behavior*, 38(2), 72.

Dilley, P. (2002). *Queer man on campus: A history of non-heterosexual college men, 1945–2000*. New York: RoutledgeFalmer.

Eliason, M. (2000). Bi-negativity: The stigma facing bisexual men. *Journal of Bisexuality*, 1(2–3), 137–154.

Fausto-Sterling, A. (2000). The five sexes, revisited. *Sciences*, 40(4), 18–23.

Ferguson, R. A. (2004). *Aberrations in black: Toward a queer of color critique*. Minneapolis, MN: University of Minnesota Press.

Foucault, M. (1978). *The history of sexuality: Vol. 1. An introduction* (R. Hurley, Trans.). New York: Vantage Books. (Originally published in 1976).

Fox, R. (1995). Bisexual identities. In A. D'Augelli & C. Patterson (Eds.), *Lesbian, gay and bisexual identities over the lifespan* (pp. 48–86). New York: Oxford University Press.

Gilley, B. J. (2006). *Becoming two-spirit: Gay identity and social acceptance in Indian country*. Lincoln, NE: University of Nebraska Press.

Halperin, D. (1997). *Saint Foucault: Towards a gay hagiography*. Oxford, UK: Oxford University Press.

Hamer, D., Wilson, J., & Florez, C. M. (2014). *Kumu hina* [Documentary].United States.: ITVS.

Kinsey, A. C., Pomeroy, W. B., & Martin, C. E. (1948). *Sexual behavior in the human male*. Bloomington, IN: Indiana University Press.

Kinsey, A. C., Pomeroy, W. B., Martin, C. E., & Gebhard, P. H. (1953). *Sexual behavior in the human female*. Bloomington, IN: Indiana University Press.

Klein, F. (1978). *The bisexual option*. Philadelphia, PA: Haworth Press.

Lev, A. I. (2004). *Transgender emergence: Therapeutic guidelines for working with gender-variant people and their families*. New York: Routledge.

MacKay, A. (Ed.). (1993). *Wolf girls at Vassar: Lesbian and gay experiences*. New York: St. Martin's Press.

Manalansan, M. (1993). (Re)locating the gay Filipino: Resistance, postcolonialism, and identity. *Journal of Homosexuality, 26*(2/3), 53–73.

Marine, S. B. (2011). Stonewall's legacy: Bisexual, gay, lesbian, and transgender students in higher education. [*ASHE Higher Education Report, 37*(4)]. San Francisco: Jossey-Bass.

Nestle, J. (1981). Butch-femme relationships: Sexual courage in the 1950s. *Heresies No. 12, 3*(4), 21–24

Nugiel, N., Goldman, W., Covington, C., Williams, B., & Leder, S. (2014). *Faking it* [Television series]. Glendora, CA: MTV.

Parks, C. W. (2001). African American same-gender-loving youths and families in urban schools. *Journal of Gay and Lesbian Social Services, 13*(3), 41–56.

Rawson, K. J., & Williams, C. (2014). Transgender∗: The rhetorical landscape of a term. *Present Tense: A Journal of Rhetoric in Society, 3*(2). Retrieved from http://www.presenttensejournal.org/volume-3/transgender-the-rhetorical-landscape-of-a-term/.

Rifkin, M. (2011). *When did Indians become straight? Kinship, the history of sexuality, and native sovereignty*. Oxford, UK: Oxford University Press.

Sansalone, D. (2013, February 25). Organisation proposes replacing the "limiting" term LGBT with "more inclusive" GSD. *Pink News*. Retrieved from http://www.pinknews.co.uk/2013/02/25/organisation-proposes-replacing-the-limiting-term-lgbt-with-more-inclusive-gsd/.

Schwartz, A. B. C. (2003). *Gay voices in the Harlem Renaissance*. Bloomington, IN: Indiana University Press.

Sell, R. L. (1996). The Sell assessment of sexual orientation: Background and scoring. *Journal of Lesbian, Gay and Bisexual Identity, 1*(4), 295–310.

Serano, J. (2007). *Whipping girl: A transsexual woman on sexism and the scapegoating of femininity*. Berkeley, CA: Seal Press.

Somerville, S. B. (2000). *Queering the color line: Race and the invention of homosexuality in American culture*. Durham, NC: Duke University Press.

Stryker, S. (2008). *Transgender history*. Berkeley, CA: Seal Press.

Tompkins, A. (2014). Asterisk. *Transgender Studies Quarterly, 1*(1–2), 26–27.

Troiden, R. R. (1979). Becoming homosexual: A model of gay identity acquisition. *Psychiatry, 42*, 362–373.

Vidal-Ortiz, S. (2011). "Maricon," "Parjaro," and "Loca": Cuban and Puerto Rican linguistic practices, and sexual minority participation, in U.S. Santeria. *Journal of Homosexuality, 58*(6–7), 901–918.

Wilson, A. (1996). How we find ourselves: Identity development in two-spirit people. *Harvard Educational Review, 66*(2), 303–317.

Wolf, S. (2009). *Sexuality and socialism: History, politics, and theory of LGBT liberation*. Chicago, IL: Haymarket Books.

T.J. JOURIAN is a PhD candidate in higher education at Loyola University Chicago.

2

This chapter describes a new model for understanding college students with minoritized identities of sexuality and gender (MIoSG) within sociopolitical, institutional/campus, homeplace, and time contexts. The MIoSG Students and Contexts Model can be adopted and adapted by educators working in a variety of postsecondary settings.

Students with Minoritized Identities of Sexuality and Gender in Campus Contexts: An Emergent Model

Annemarie Vaccaro, E. I. Annie Russell, Robert M. Koob

We begin this chapter by discussing some of the challenges to understanding the identities, demographics, and campus experiences of students with *minoritized identities of sexuality and gender* (MIoSG). Building upon campus climate models, Bronfenbrenner's bioecological model, and empirical literature about college students with MIoSG, we present a new MIoSG Students and Contexts Model that can be used by educators in various postsecondary institutional contexts to understand and support students with MIoSG.

In this chapter, we use MIoSG because choosing particular identities in the LGBTQ acronym (for example, gay, lesbian, bisexual, transgender) excludes and normalizes groups of people. We follow the increasingly common practice of an interdisciplinary community of scholars (such as Benitez, 2010; Chase, Dowd, Pazich, & Bensimon, 2014; Gillborn, 2005; Godard, Mukjerjee, & Mukherjee, 2006; Patton, Harper, & Harris, 2015) to use the term *minoritized* as we discuss those whose sexuality and gender have been consigned to lower status, visibility, and power.

Although we intentionally selected MIoSG for our prose, we use versions of the LGBTQ acronym to honor names, titles, and terminology choices of other authors.

Student Identities and Demographics

Despite the increase in research about gender and sexuality in higher education, we have limited knowledge about the identities, demographics, and

NEW DIRECTIONS FOR STUDENT SERVICES, no. 152, Winter 2015 © 2015 Wiley Periodicals, Inc.
Published online in Wiley Online Library (wileyonlinelibrary.com) • DOI: 10.1002/ss.20143

campus experiences of students with minoritized identities of sexuality and gender at various types of postsecondary institutions. Self-identification is a critical aspect of understanding students with MIoSG in higher education. Providing opportunities for students with MIoSG to self-identify allows institutions of higher education to effectively track, support, and affirm students with MIoSG. However, the common application, used by more than 500 colleges and universities, does not ask about sexual orientation or gender identity. In our own research we found 39 institutions of higher education have begun to ask more inclusive demographic questions by encouraging students with MIoSG to self-identify in two distinct capacities: through admissions and registration. The first institution to do this was Elmhurst College in 2011 through its application for admission (Stoller, 2011). When this chapter was written, three undergraduate institutions (Elmhurst College, Massachusetts Institute of Technology, and the University of Iowa) as well as three law schools (University of Pennsylvania, Boston University, and University of Washington) gathered sexuality and gender demographics on their admission applications. In 2013, presidents of the entire Washington State 2-year college system made the unanimous decision to begin gathering sexuality and gender demographics through students' registration processes, which allows those schools to capture self-identity changes over time.

Despite advancements at these institutions, there are limitations that hinder our knowledge about the total number and evolving self-identifications of students with MIoSG. First, these schools represent only a handful of the more than 4,000 institutions in the United States. Second, the phrasing of the questions and response options are vastly different at these campuses, making data comparisons difficult. For instance, Elmhurst College broadly asked students if they identified as members of the LGBT community whereas Washington State's 2-year system asked students their sexual orientation and gender identity (Ingeno, 2013; Stoller, 2011). Finally, because efforts to collect these data are new, there is little agreement concerning the utility of the data and how to effectively support students with MIoSG with the information.

Campus Contexts for Students with MIoSG

In line with this volume's emphasis on Bronfenbrenner's (1993) bioecological model, we contend it is impossible to understand college students with MIoSG without considering institutional context—namely type. Beginning in 1970, the Carnegie Commission on Higher Education began classifying postsecondary institutions by type. The classifications have undergone revisions over the years and were undergoing a major revision at the time this chapter was written. As of July 2014, the classification variables used to distinguish among postsecondary institutions included basic classification, undergraduate program, graduate program, enrollment profile, size and setting, community engagement, geographic region, level of institution, control of institution, degree of urbanization, and accreditation type. Classification variables also included whether a school was a historically Black college and university (HBCU), tribal college, women's college, Hispanic serving institution (HSI), minority serving institution, urban institution, institution with a medical school, or a Council of Public Liberal Arts (COPLAC) institution.

Research about the development and experiences of students with MIoSG has mostly been conducted at large, 4-year institutions and has been primarily concentrated on students who identify as some combination of lesbian, gay, or bisexual. Research conducted at large 4-year public schools is too extensive to address in this chapter. However, it is important to acknowledge the vastness of this literature, which covers topics such as identity development; relationships with peers, faculty, and staff; engagement in MIoSG-specific campus resources/organizations; and experiences with heterosexism and homophobia (Abes & Jones, 2004; Abes & Kasch, 2007; Bilodeau, 2005; D'Augelli, 1992, 1994; Evans & Broido, 1999, 2002; McKinney, 2005; Peña-Talamantes, 2013; Renn & Bilodeau, 2005; Stevens, 2004).

Scholars have begun to conduct research on students with MIoSG at more varied institutional types. Patton (2011) and Patton and Simmons (2008) conducted research about the experiences of students with MIoSG at historically Black colleges and universities. Two studies have been conducted at women's colleges, where Holland and Holley (2011) examined gay White men's experiences and Hart and Lester (2011) captured transgender students' experiences. Only a few published studies have been done about the experiences of students with MIoSG at private, religiously affiliated institutions (see Love, 1997; Patton & Simmons, 2008). Our review revealed a dearth of empirical research conducted about the experiences of students with MIoSG at tribal colleges, community colleges, or other specialized institutions (for example, seminaries, medical schools, professional schools).

In response to the gap in our understanding about students with MIoSG at various institutional types, we infused campus and other contextual forces into the MIoSG Students and Contexts Model. As readers will see in Figure 2.1, institutional context (including type) comprises a significant part of the model. However, it is not the *only* influence on students with MIoSG. We contend that by taking a holistic view of self and contexts we can best understand the complex realities of students with MIoSG in postsecondary education.

As discussed in Chapter One, understanding of identity and development for students with MIoSG in higher education has changed drastically since the late 1970s. Considering the field's evolution from stage-based,

Figure 2.1. MIoSG Students and Contexts

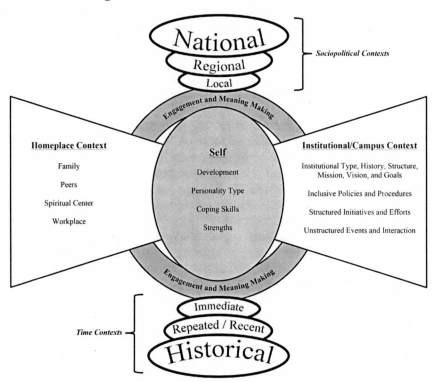

linear models to more nuanced understandings of how identity is coconstructed within the context of environment, it is crucial to examine what is known about the campus climate experiences of students with MIoSG. A number of studies have documented unwelcoming and hostile campus climates and microclimates for people with MIoSG, as well as unique manifestations of exclusion by gender, gender identity, race, and role on campus (Rankin, 2003; Rankin, Weber, Blumenfeld, & Frazer, 2010; Vaccaro, 2012). As we crafted our model, we considered climate descriptions from these studies as well as foundational works operationalizing campus climate (Hurtado & Guillermo-Wann, 2013; Hurtado, Milem, Clayton-Pederson, & Allen, 1998; Milem, Chang, & antonio, 2005; Renn & Arnold, 2003).

Hurtado et al. (1998) identified the following as critical factors in measuring and understanding campus climate with respect to diverse people (particularly through the lenses of race and ethnicity): historical legacy of inclusion or exclusion, structural diversity, psychological dimension of climate, behavioral dimension of climate, and implications for policy and practice within each of these. Renn and Arnold (2003) used Bronfenbrenner's (1993) bioecological model as a tool for understanding peer culture and how it influenced students' understanding of self. Hurtado et al. (2008) and Milem et al. (2005) situated the factors for diverse campus climate measurement in a model to further extrapolate how these dimensions fit together. Finally, Hurtado and Guillermo-Wann (2013) reconceptualized a model for understanding climate and diverse populations from two dimensions to three to reflect dynamics of power and dimensions of hierarchical influences. Although some of the diverse climate issues in these models affect students with MIoSG on campus, others seem far less relevant. Also, specific factors addressed in the empirical literature on students with MIoSG did not seem to fit with, or appear in, some of these climate models. As such, we turned to Bronfenbrenner (1993) to more fully examine the application of the bioecological model to MIoSG students.

As discussed in the Editors' Notes for this sourcebook, Bronfenbrenner (1993) bioecological model includes the microsystem, mesosystem, exosystem, and macrosystem as tools for understanding how people develop through interactions with surrounding environmental influences. Although Bronfenbrenner's model (1993) can be used as an effective overlay for any system, we believed that, by itself, it did not do justice to the intricate pieces of the campus climate context or the unique developmental processes that MIoSG students face in institutions of higher education. As such, we propose a new MIoSG Students in Context Model that builds upon the most relevant aspects of campus climate models and Bronfenbrenner work, as well as empirical research about MIoSG college student experiences and identities.

Students with MIoSG and Contexts: A New Model

In the following pages, we present a new framework that can be used by educators who work with MIoSG students in a variety of postsecondary settings. In Figure 2.1, the center of the MIoSG Students in Context Model represents an individual's holistic sense of self. We use the word "holistic" to push traditional boundaries of "identities" that, in most research studies, are limited to identity statuses, stages, or phases related to psychosocial, cognitive-structural, and moral identity models without regard to other important factors that shape a sense of self. A review of these models is outside the scope of this chapter but can be found elsewhere (see Evans, Forney, Guido, Patton, & Renn, 2010). The circle at the center of our model represents the "sense of self" and contains not only traditional perspectives on development but also personality type, strengths, and coping skills.

In addition to developmental locations, a student's sense of self can be related to personality and preferred styles of interaction. Carl Jung (1923/1971) explained how individuals respond to the same environment (for example, campus) differently based upon variations in their interests, mode of information processing, and ideal learning style. Jung's work inspired Myers (1980) to develop the Myers-Briggs Type Inventory, which measures personality type along four dimensions: extraversion/introversion, sensing/intuition, thinking/feeling, and judging/perceiving. Where an individual falls on each of these spectrums shapes how they absorb information from their environment, process it, and then act. For example, an extroverted, sensing, thinking, and judging (ESTJ) student with MIoSG at a particular type of school (for example, large faith-related institution, tribal college, midsized rural community college) may perceive, experience, and respond to the campus in a very different way than an introverted, intuitive, feeling, and perceiving (INFP) student with MIoSG on that same campus.

In alignment with this volume's rejection of deficit-model thinking, our model includes strengths as an important aspect of self. In general, strengths could refer to an individual's skills, abilities, and talents as well as the level of confidence that accompanies those strengths. More specifically, strengths can be understood by the 34 themes of talent measured by the Clifton StrengthsFinder® tool. These talents are "recurring patterns of thought, feeling, or behavior that can be productively applied" and can be developed into a strength if honed into a consistent pattern of performance (Gallup Inc., 2009, p. 34). An individual's top five talents can shape the way she/ze/he/they responds to welcoming campus climates or hostility from peers, faculty, and staff.

The final aspect of self is coping skills, which refers to the tactics people use to deal with stressful situations. Literature about the higher education experiences of MIoSG students is replete with narratives of heterosexism, genderism, homophobia, and transphobia (Bilodeau, 2009; D'Augelli, 1992; D'Augelli & Rose, 1990; Rankin, 2003; Rankin et al., 2010). We believe the capacity to cope effectively with exclusion is a central aspect of self, especially for minoritized populations. Yet, very little literature emphasizes the resilience and coping mechanisms students use to respond to oppression. In focus groups with individuals from a variety of minoritized social identity groups, Iwasaki, Bartlett, MacKay, Mactavish, and Ristock (2008) found gay and lesbian participants coped by reframing stress and discrimination as character-building experiences and opportunities to learn and grow. In an ethnographic study with nine diverse trans*[1] college students, Nicolazzo (2015) described how they drew support from kinship networks to navigate the gender binary discourse and compulsory heterogenderism, the conflation of sexual identities with gender identities, on campus. We contend that

---

[1] As explained by T.J. Jourian in his chapter in this volume, "The asterisk at the end of the prefix trans is used to signal broad inclusivity of multiple gender identities beyond just trans men (also referred to as female-to-male or transgender men) or trans women (also referred to as male-to-female or transgender women), such as nonbinary individuals, as well as crossdressers and even gender performers like drag kings and queens (Tompkins, 2014)."

coping skills and strategies used by students with MIoSG can be an important aspect of their sense of self and manner in which they navigate isms on and off campus.

Surrounding the center circle of the model are overlapping discs and two trapezoids that represent contextual factors influencing the individual's sense of self and their daily experiences. The overlapping discs at the top of the model, labeled sociopolitical contexts have roots in Bronfenbrenner (1993) macrosystem and exosystyem. We overlapped the discs to draw attention to the interconnections among national, regional, and local sociopolitical contexts. The top disc is the national context, which refers to the economic, historical, political, and cultural context of any nation state. Although much of our emphasis is on the United States, the contexts of other countries can also influence how students with MIoSG (in the United States and abroad) feel about themselves. For instance, news about exclusionary policies or state-sanctioned human rights violations (for example, the execution of people with MIoSG) or affirming policies (for example, same-gender marriage) could send powerful messages to individuals about what it means to be minoritized by sexuality and gender in global contexts. In the United States, the lack of affirmative federal legislation (for example, nondiscrimination protection) can influence how people with MIoSG understand themselves and move through the world. The cognitive and emotional impacts of living in a nation that fails to offer equal rights and regularly engages in heated debates about those rights cannot be understated.

The next disc downward is the regional context, which refers loosely to both geographic regions (for example, New England, Great Lakes, Plains; Carnegie Classification of Institutions of Higher Education, 2014) of the United States and individual states. Each state has a different mix of laws that govern the lives of people with MIoSG. College students whose home or college is located in a state with nondiscrimination clauses (inclusive of sexual orientation and gender identity), same-gender marriage, school antibullying policies, joint adoption laws, and hospital visitation laws may be more apt to develop a positive sense of self and experience less overt marginalization than someone growing up or studying in a state with explicit anti-MIoSG legislation.

The disc at the final level down in sociopolitical contexts is local. This can include city ordinances and the presence (or lack) of inclusive spiritual communities, LGBT community agencies, and activist groups for people with MIoSG. For instance, a college student living in a town with marriage prohibition or gender policing policies might receive very different messages about self than one living in a community with strong LGBT youth organizations, active PFLAG chapters, affirming churches, and regular community celebrations such as pride parades. These two students may also have differential access to safe community spaces where they can explore their identities and find support systems.

The overlapping discs at the bottom of the model represent the context of time. Bronfenbrenner and Morris (1998) delved deeply into the significance of different types of time: microtime includes the brief time during an interaction or activity, mesotime refers to the recurrent patterns of interactions or activities, and macrotime references the influence of major social events that occur at different points in history. An adaptation of these perspectives on time can be found in our model. The largest disc at the bottom of the model represents historical events, especially those related to MIoSG people's civil rights. For instance, sense of self for nontraditional age MIoSG learners whose lives were touched by historical events such as the Stonewall Riots (1969), the murder of Matthew Shepard (1998), and the Defense of Marriage Act's passage (1996) and/or dismantling (2011–2013) may be quite different from younger MIoSG students for whom these events are purely historical.

The next concept of time (represented by the middle disc) includes "recent/repeated" events. Examples of recent events might include a trans∗ awareness campus event that happened last week or a hate crime that occurred in the local community 6 months ago. Repeated events can include campus/community celebrations and vigils such as Transgender Remembrance Day or National Coming Out Day, as well as regularly scheduled queer student organization meetings or educational programs about MIoSG people and issues.

The final time context includes immediate happenings, which are represented by the smallest disc in this set. Sense of self and campus experiences for students with MIoSG are shaped by the present. When a classmate utters a derogatory term, a faculty member confronts (or ignores) bias, or a staff member uses MIoSG-affirmative language, an individual's sense of self and campus experience can be immediately influenced. Immediate happenings can also include publicized campus events such as speakers who identify with MIoSG, research presentations by faculty with MIoSG, or student protests.

The left portion of the model is titled homeplace context. Gouthro (2005) argued that homeplace is the first site of learning about self and the world. She pushed the bounds of heteronormative and limited geographic notions of home when describing homeplace as a phenomenon with affective and/or physical dimensions. Homeplace can include an abode as well as sociocultural relations with kin, neighbors, or members of a cultural community. Building upon Gouthro's work, we framed the homeplace context broadly to include off-campus people and places important to college students. These entities include family, peers, spiritual centers, and workplaces.

As noted by Gouthro, family can have various meanings, especially for individuals with MIoSG. We refer to family as those who are not chosen by an individual (for example, biological, legal) as well as chosen kin—considered family without biological or legal ties. We contend that historical, recent, and current interactions with chosen and unchosen families can have a profound impact on sense of self and daily functioning in a collegiate environment. With a rise in students over the age of 25 (Snyder & Dillow, 2011) as well as the sheer number of campuses that offer little or no campus housing, many college students reside off campus. It is unknown how many of these students live with families of origin, extended kin, or chosen families. But students may connect with their families, regardless of how they define them, on a regular basis. This may be especially true for students from collectivist community origins. As such, we have included family as an important force in the homeplace context.

The homeplace context also includes peers with whom people with MIoSG interact in structured (for example, classrooms, teams, clubs) and unstructured (in other words, neighborhoods, hallways, cyberconnectivity) community and school settings. Both direct and indirect interactions with supportive and unsupportive peers are paramount to a sense of self. In line with our model that emphasizes various time contexts, we believe focusing exclusively on current campus relationships minimizes the influence of positive and negative relations from a student's past or present homeplace context.

The third aspect of the homeplace context is the spiritual center. As a result of exclusive interpretations of religious texts, many people with MIoSG have felt marginalized by faith communities (Vaccaro, August, & Kennedy, 2012). Others, however, have found community and support in LGBT-affirming religious and spiritual centers (Vaccaro et al., 2012). We contend religious and spiritual experiences across an individual's lifetime can have profound effects on his or her holistic sense of self and experiences in college.

The final aspect of the homeplace is the workplace. An overwhelming majority of college students work paid jobs while attending college (Perna, 2010). Whether they are employed full or part time, a workplace can influence a student's ability to pay for college and promote the development of various forms of human, social, and cultural capital. Workplace settings can be powerful microclimates (Vaccaro, 2012) where MIoSG people receive affirmative or exclusionary messages from coworkers, supervisors, clients, and the physical environment. Consider the differences in a work environment that consistently hosts safe zone trainings, compared to one where supervisors and coworkers regularly tell (or ignore) "gay jokes" or require students to wear nametags with only their legal name. In sum, on and off campus work settings can be influential contextual factors for MIoSG students' sense of self and collegiate reality.

The trapezoid comprising the right portion of the model represents institutional and campus context. Institutional type is one very important aspect of the model. However, as we described earlier, there is a constantly changing list of institutional types (Carnegie Classification, 2014). All of the variables listed in the Carnegie Classifications can influence the mission, vision, and goals of an organization. These guiding documents reflect the current and future focus of a university and, when enacted appropriately, should influence all decision making. Enacted missions, visions, and goal statements that describe a commitment to social justice or affirm the diversity of community members may be reflective of very different campus environments than in schools that do not have such declarations. Also, mission, vision, and goal statements with exclusionary language (for example, male/female, sexual preference, homosexuality) can send powerful messages to students with MIoSG. It is important to remember there are similarities *and* differences among institutions that share a classification (for example, tribal colleges, associates/community colleges, liberal arts institutions, schools of music or design, research intensive institutions). Therefore, it is impossible to draw generalizable conclusions about the experiences of, and identity influences on, people with MIoSG by institutional type. Instead, practitioners must consider institutional type in conjunction with a host of other environmental variables. For instance, institutional history matters. A school with a history of exclusion or inclusion might feel quite different to students with MIoSG. Institutional structure also matters. A campus with a staffed and funded LGBTQ center, support groups for MIoSG, recognized associations for students and faculty/staff with MIoSG, and Queer Studies programs will send different messages to students with MIoSG than campuses without such structures.

Other scholars have documented the importance of inclusive policies and procedures in creating affirming campus environments (Zemsky & Sanlo, 2005) and/or organizational change (Hornsby, 2006). We agree that policies and procedures are vital to the ways students make meaning of themselves in the context of their campus environment. MIoSG-affirming policies and procedures can include sexual orientation and gender-inclusive nondiscrimination statements, preferred first name and pronoun change processes, and zero tolerance antibullying policies. Gender-inclusive health insurance plans for students and employees that cover primary care, gynecological and urological care, reproductive options and family planning, voice and communication therapy, mental health services (for example, assessment, counseling, psychotherapy), hormone replacement therapy, and gender confirmation surgery are also very important. Colleges, like those cited in the opening section of this chapter, with standard policies about asking *and* honoring changes in self-identification can send affirming messages to students with MIoSG. Additional inclusive policies and processes allow students to use restrooms and locker rooms and select residence hall rooms based upon their gender identity instead of assigned/legal sex. Campus policies regarding the process of creating and offering Queer Studies (and other MIoSG-inclusive) courses across the curriculum are also critically important. If such courses face challenging approval processes, or are relegated to elective-only credit, they are not infused into the central structure of the university, and thus, can be deemed tangential and unimportant. In turn, MIoSG students can feel tangential and unimportant.

Another essential element of the institutional context includes structured initiatives such as educational programs, cultural events, and social activities. Such efforts might include those tailored for a particular institutional context (for example, women's college, medical school) or broad-based initiatives adopted from national campaigns, such as *Stop the Hate*, *It Gets Better*, *You Can Play*, and safe zone programs. In the prior section, we mentioned the importance of structural support for MIoSG-centered curriculum. Here, we argue that the delivery, outcomes, and reputation of MIoSG-inclusive courses also contribute to the holistic sense of self and campus experiences for students with MIoSG. Students who see themselves positively reflected in curriculum may be affected differently than those for whom curriculum is absent of positive images of people and topics related to MIoSG. A final aspect of structured initiatives relates to physical space on campus. Is there affirmative signage on campus (for example, safe zone signs, inclusive language) or the presence of visible and centrally located queer/LGBT/gender/sexuality center? If there is a center or office, is it staffed by full-time employees? Such structural and environmental factors are important to the experiences of students with MIoSG on campus.

Finally, unstructured events and interactions also shape the campus context. Hearing a classmate tell a homophobic joke, witnessing a staff member make fun of a trans∗ colleague, seeing offensive graffiti, or listening to binary/exclusionary language from campus leaders contributes to the institutional context. Conversely, spontaneous pro-MIoSG rallies, affirming social media posts from university departments, inclusive classroom discussions, and peers who invite others to use preferred gender pronouns shape the institutional context in a more positive way. Visibility of out faculty and staff with MIoSG, who can serve as role models and mentors, also shapes the informal and unstructured aspects of a campus context.

The final part of the model is the engagement and meaning-making ring that connects the self to the four outer components of the model. Engagement refers to the reciprocal interactions between the self and contexts over time. This portion of our model was informed by the concept of proximal processes: "Human development takes place through processes of progressively more complex reciprocal interaction between an active, evolving biopsychological human organism and the persons, objects, and symbols in its immediate external environment" (Bronfenbrenner & Morris, 1998, p. 996). Building upon the concept of proximal processes, we added the constructivist notion of meaning making. It is not merely an experience or reciprocal interaction that contributes to an individual's evolving sense of self, but how they process and understand that event in the context of their past and present realities. Constructivist developmental theories recognize human beings as active agents who are "consistently engaged in constructing knowledge, imposing meaning, organization, and structure upon experience" (Popp & Portnow, 2001, p. 53). This ring connects each component of the model, highlighting how students with MIoSG make meaning of themselves through engagement with campus, sociopolitical, homeplace, and time contexts. This person-centered and contextually situated meaning-making process can help educators understand how students with MIoSG, even at the same institution, make meaning of a campus policy, initiative, or interaction in vastly different ways.

Conclusion

In the opening segments of this chapter, we described how little is known about the identities, demographics, and campus experiences of students with MIoSG at different types of institutions. Drawing upon campus climate literature, Bronfenbrenner's bioecological model, and research about college students with MIoSG, we developed the MIoSG Students in Campus Context Model. We contend the manner in which college students with MIoSG make meaning of their identities and campus experiences is shaped by institutional context, homeplace, sociopolitical systems, and time. We hope educators will find the MIoSG Students in Campus Context Model a useful tool for understanding and supporting students with MIoSG on their particular campus.

References

Abes, E. S., & Jones, S. R. (2004). Meaning-making capacity and the dynamics of lesbian college students' multiple dimensions of identity. *Journal of College Student Development, 45*(6), 612—632.

Abes, E. S., & Kasch, D. (2007). Using queer theory to explore lesbian college students' multiple dimensions of identity. *Journal of College Student Development, 48*(6), 619–636.

Benitez, M. (2010). Resituating culture centers within a social justice framework: Is there room for examining whiteness? In L. Patton (Ed.), *Culture centers in higher education: Perspectives on identity, theory, and practice* (pp. 119–136). Sterling, VA: Stylus.

Bilodeau, B. (2005). Beyond the gender binary: A case study of two transgender students at a midwestern research university. *Journal of Gay & Lesbian Issues in Education, 3*(1), 29–44.

Bilodeau, B. (2009). *Genderism: Transgender students, binary systems, and higher education.* Saarbrücken, Germany: VDM Verlag Dr. Müller.

Bronfenbrenner, U. (1993). The ecology of cognitive development: Research models and fugitive findings. In R. H. Wozniak & K. W. Fischer (Eds.), *Development in context: Acting and thinking in specific environments* (pp. 3–44). Hillsdale, NJ: Erlbaum.

Bronfenbrenner, U., & Morris, P. A. (1998). The ecology of developmental processes. In W. Damon & R. M. Lerner (Eds.), *Handbook of child psychology, Vol. 1: Theoretical models of human development* (5th ed., pp. 993–1023). New York: Wiley.

Carnegie Classification of Institutions of Higher Education™. (2014). *Carnegie Classifications data file*. Retrieved from http://carnegieclassifications.iu.edu/resources/.

Chase, M. M., Dowd, A. C., Pazich, L. B., & Bensimon, E. M. (2014). Transfer equity for "minoritized" students: A critical policy analysis of seven states. *Educational Policy*, 28(5), 669–717.

D'Augelli, A. R. (1992). Lesbian and gay male undergraduates' experiences of harassment and fear on campus. *Journal of Interpersonal Violence*, 7(3), 383–395.

D'Augelli, A. R. (1994). Identity development and sexual orientation: Toward a model of lesbian, gay, and bisexual development. In E. J. Trickett, R. J. Watts, & D. Birman (Eds.), *Human diversity: Perspectives on people in context* (pp. 312–333). San Francisco, CA: Jossey-Bass.

D'Augelli, A. R., & Rose, M. L. (1990). Homophobia in a university community: Attitudes and experiences of white, heterosexual freshman. *Journal of College Student Development*, 31(6), 484–491.

Evans, N. J., & Broido, E. M. (1999). Coming out in the residence halls: Negotiation, meaning making, challenges, supports. *Journal of College Student Development*, 40(6), 658–668.

Evans, N. J., & Broido, E. M. (2002). The experiences of lesbian and bisexual women in college residence halls. *Journal of Lesbian Studies*, 6(3–4), 29–42.

Evans, N. J., Forney, D., Guido, F, Patton, L. D., & Renn, K. A. (2010). *Student development in college* (2nd ed.). San Francisco, CA: Jossey-Bass.

Gallup Inc. (2009). *StrengthsQuest Educator Seminar*. Washington,DC: Gallup Inc.

Gillborn, D. (2005). Education policy as an act of white supremacy: Whiteness, critical race theory and education reform. *Journal of Education Policy*, 20(4), 485–505.

Godard, B. J., Mukjerjee, A. P., & Mukherjee, A. (2006). Translating minoritized cultures: Issues of caste, class and gender. *Postcolonial Text*, 2(3), 1–23.

Gouthro, P. A. (2005). A critical feminist analysis of the homeplace as learning site: Expanding the discourse of lifelong learning to consider adult women learners. *International Journal of lifelong education*, 24(1), 5–19.

Hart, J., & Lester, J. (2011). Starring students: Gender performance at a women's college. *NASPA Journal about Women in Higher Education*, 4(2), 193–217.

Holland, C., & Holley, K., (2011). The experiences of gay male undergraduate students at a traditional women's college. *Journal of Student Affairs Research and Practice*, 48(2), 179–194.

Hornsby, E. E. (2006, Winter). Using policy to drive organizational change. In R. J. Hill (Ed.), *New Directions for Adult and Continuing Education: No. 112. Challenging homophobia and heterosexism: Lesbian, gay, bisexual, transgender, and queer issues in organizational settings* (pp. 73–83). San Francisco, CA: Jossey-Bass.

Hurtado, S., & Guillermo-Wann, C. (2013). *Diverse learning environments: Assessing and creating conditions for student success—final report to the Ford Foundation*. University of California, Los Angeles: Higher Education Research Institute.

Hurtado, S., Milem, J. F., Clayton-Pederson, A. R., & Allen, W. R. (1998). Enhancing campus climates for racial/ethnic diversity: Educational policy and practice. *The Review of Higher Education*, 21(3), 279–302.

Ingeno, L. (2013). *Ask, do tell*. Retrieved from https://www.insidehighered.com/news/2013/08/05/washington-state-2-year-colleges-will-ask-students-about-sexual-orientation.

Iwasaki, Y., Bartlett, J., MacKay, K., Mactavish, J., & Ristock, J. (2008). Mapping non-dominant voices into understanding stress-coping mechanisms. *Journal of Community Psychology*, 36(6), 702–722.

Jung, C. G. (1971). *The collected works of C. G. Jung* (Vol. 6., R.F.C. Hull, Ed. & H.G. Baynes Trans) Princeton, NJ: Princeton University Press. (Original work published in 1923).

Love, P. (1997). Contradiction and paradox: Attempting to change the culture of sexual orientation at a small Catholic college. *Review of Higher Education, 20*(4), 381–398.

McKinney, J. S. (2005). On the margins: A study of the experiences of transgender college students. *Journal of Gay & Lesbian Issues in Education, 3*(1), 63–76.

Milem, J. F., Chang, M. J., & antonio, a. l. (2005). *Making diversity work on campus: A research-based perspective.* Washington, DC: American Association of Colleges and Universities.

Myers, I. B. (1980). *Gifts differing.* Palo Alto, CA; Consulting Psychologists Press.

Nicolazzo, Z. (2015). *"Just go in looking good": The resilience, resistance, and kinship-building of trans* college students.* Electronic dissertation, Miami University. Retrieved from https://etd.ohiolink.edu/.

Patton, L. D. (2011). Perspectives on identity, disclosure, and the campus environment among African American gay and bisexual college men at one historically black college. *Journal of College Student Development, 52*(1), 77–100.

Patton, L. D., & Simmons, S. L. (2008). Exploring complexities of multiple identities of lesbians in a black college environment. *The Negro Educational Review, 59*(3–4), 197–215.

Patton, L. D., Harper, S. R., & Harris, J. (2015). Using critical race theory to (re)interpret widely studied topics related to U.S. higher education. In A. M. Martinez-Alemán, B. Pusser, & E. M. Bensimon (Eds.), *Critical approaches to the study of higher education: A practical introduction* (pp. 193–219). Baltimore, MD: Johns Hopkins University.

Peña-Talamantes, A.E., (2013). Empowering the self, creating worlds: Lesbian and gay Latina/o college students' identity negotiation in figured worlds. *Journal of College Student Development, 54*(3), 267–282.

Perna, L. W. (2010). *Understanding the working college student: New research and its implications for policy and practice.* Sterling, VA: Stylus.

Popp, N., & Portnow, K. (2001). Our developmental perspective on adulthood. In Adult Development Research Group (Ed.), *Toward a new pluralism in ABE/ESOL classrooms: Teaching to multiple "cultures if mind"* (pp. 43–75). Cambridge, MA: National Center for Adult Learning and Literacy.

Rankin, S. (2003). *Campus climate for gay, lesbian, bisexual and transgender people: A national perspective.* New York, NY: National Gay and Lesbian Task Force Policy Institute.

Rankin, S., Weber, G., Blumenfeld, W., & Frazer, S. (2010). *2010 state of higher education for lesbian, gay, bisexual & transgender people.* Charlotte, NC: Campus Pride.

Renn, K. A., & Arnold, K. D. (2003). Reconceptualizing research on peer culture. *Journal of Higher Education, 74,* 261–291.

Renn, K. A., & Bilodeau, B. (2005). Queer student leaders: An exploratory case study of identity development and LGBT student involvement at a midwestern research university. *Journal of Gay & Lesbian Issues in Education, 2*(4), 49–71.

Snyder, T. D., & Dillow, S.A. (2011). *Digest of education statistics 2010* (NCES 2011–015). Washington, DC: U.S. Department of Education, National Center for Education Statistics. Retrieved from http://nces.ed.gov/pubs2011/2011015.pdf.

Stevens, R. A., Jr., (2004). Understanding gay identity development within the college environment. *Journal of College Student Development, 45*(2), 185–206.

Stoller, E. (2011, August 24). *Elmhurst College adds sexual orientation and gender identity to admissions process* [Web blog post]. Retrieved from https://www.insidehighered.com/blogs/student_affairs_and_technology/elmhurst_college_adds_sexual_orientation_and_gender_identity_to_admissions_process.

Tompkins, A. (2014). Asterisk. *Transgender Studies Quarterly, 1*(1–2), 26–27.

Vaccaro, A. (2012). Campus microclimates for LGBT faculty, staff, and students: An exploration of the intersections of social identity and campus roles. *Journal of Student Affairs Research and Practice, 49*(4), 359–480.

Vaccaro, A., August, G., & Kennedy, M. S. (2012). *Safe spaces: Making schools and communities welcoming to LGBT youth.* Santa Barbara, CA: Praeger.
Zemsky, B., & Sanlo, R. L. (2005, Fall). Do policies matter? In R. Sanlo (Ed.), *New Directions for Student Services: No. 111. Gender identity and sexual orientation: Research policy and personal perspectives* (pp. 7–16). San Francisco, CA: Jossey-Bass.

ANNEMARIE VACCARO is an Aassociate professor in the College Student Personnel Program at the University of Rhode Island.

E. I. ANNIE RUSSELL is director of the Gender and Sexuality Center at the University of Rhode Island.

ROBERT M. KOOB is a master's degree student in the College Student Personnel Program at the University of Rhode Island.

3

This chapter examines curricula as important microsystems for LGBTQ college students. The authors explore sociocultural influences on curricula and discuss strategies for creating positive curricular experiences for LGBTQ students.

LGBTQ Experiences in Curricular Contexts

Jodi L. Linley, David J. Nguyen

Well-known theorists of college student attrition (for example, Astin, 1993; Tinto, 1987, 1993) emphasize the importance of social and academic integration for students into postsecondary education. Academic integration occurs within complex curricular contexts that serve as important microsystems for college students. Curricular contexts are subject to macrosystem and exosystem forces, such as historical events, state policies, and disciplinary culture (Lattuca & Stark, 2009). For example, many curricular contexts are influenced by state funding models. Administrators, faculty, and staff experience pressure to meet certain performance criteria in order to receive varying levels of state funding. This pressure influences student recruitment and enrollment, student services practices, and curricular decisions.

To visualize curricular contexts within an ecological model, we use Lattuca and Stark's (2009) Academic Plan Model. In their model, curricula are conceptualized as dynamic sites of interaction among learners, instructors, and content that are subject to external and internal sociocultural influences (Lattuca & Stark, 2009; see Figure 1). For this chapter, we define *curricular contexts* as academic experiences and interactions among lesbian, gay, bisexual, transgender and queer (LGBTQ) learners, instructors, and content as they are influenced by sociocultural external and internal forces. The need to understand LGBTQ curricular contexts stems from research that suggests heterosexism, genderism, homophobia, and transphobia are a normative reality on contemporary college campuses (Bilodeau, 2009; Rankin, Weber, Blumenfeld, & Frazer, 2010). Hatzenbuehler (2009) posited that when LGBTQ individuals experience exposure to stress as a result of stigma, they are at greater risk for difficulties with emotional regulation, interpersonal relationships, and negative cognitions. One way LGBTQ individuals cope

NEW DIRECTIONS FOR STUDENT SERVICES, no. 152, Winter 2015 © 2015 Wiley Periodicals, Inc.
Published online in Wiley Online Library (wileyonlinelibrary.com) • DOI: 10.1002/ss.20144

with such stigma is by remaining "closeted" (in other words, not disclosing or correcting false assumptions about their true identities) (Bilimoria & Stewart, 2009; LaSala, Jenkins, Wheeler, & Fredriksen-Goldsen, 2008). LGBTQ students experiencing this enhanced marginalization may not persist, similar to the effects of racial microaggressions on students of color. This chapter seeks to spark conversation and motivation among college educators to create positive curricular environments for LGBTQ students so that they may not experience stigmatization, but instead experience their collegiate environments as safe and supportive of their LGBTQ identities.

Sociocultural Influences on LGBTQ Curricular Contexts

Examining curricular contexts provides an opportunity to explore the ways that LGBTQ individuals experience these contexts. For example, how might institutional antidiscrimination policies influence the ways trans*[1] students experience curricula? Might gay and lesbian students experience curricula differently based on the sexual orientation of their faculty or instructors? Are there differences in the curricular contexts of LGBTQ students in varying academic disciplines? In this section, we review literature about external and internal influences on curricula for LGBTQ individuals. It is of note that these influences are not independent of each other; rather, they are interrelated influences on students' overall curricular experiences.

External Influences on LGBTQ Curricular Contexts.   Lattuca and Stark (2009) identified a variety of external influences on curricula, such as market forces, accrediting agencies, and government policies. Two external influences related to LGBTQ curricular contexts are the potential emergence of a "post-LGBTQ" era and disciplinary norms.

Potential Emergence of a "Post-LGBTQ" Era.   The year 2014 saw the first openly gay man running for governor of a U.S. state, 35 U.S. states with marriage equality and another 10 pending rulings, multiple television series featuring LGBTQ celebrities and characters, and openly gay athletes in numerous professional sports. With these examples of LGBTQ integration into mainstream society, it is tempting to assume we are living in a "post-LGBTQ" era. In fact, some consider today's college-going population to be experiencing a "postgay" society (for example, Ghaziani, 2011; sollender, 2011). But data tell a different story and presently, the mainstream narrative of LGBTQ culture remains largely White and cisgender (meaning individuals whose gender identity conforms with their biological sex); people of color and trans* individuals continue to be underrepresented

---

[1]As explained by T.J. Jourian in his chapter in this volume, "The asterisk at the end of the prefix trans is used to signal broad inclusivity of multiple gender identities beyond just trans men (also referred to as female-to-male or transgender men) or trans women (also referred to as male-to-female or transgender women), such as nonbinary individuals, as well as crossdressers and even gender performers like drag kings and queens (Tompkins, 2014)."

(Ng, 2013). In a recent report, 87% of anti-LGBTQ murder victims were people of color and 45% of hate murders were transgender women (National Coalition of Anti-Violence Programs, 2012). Further, more than 50% of trans∗ youth attempt suicide at least once by age 20 (Youth Suicide Prevention Program, 2014). In 2014, in 31 U.S. states no laws prohibit discrimination based on gender identity, and the same is true in 29 states regarding sexual orientation (Human Rights Campaign, 2014); nor is discrimination explicitly prohibited by federal law. It follows from these data that we are *not* living in a "post-LGBTQ" society.

Academic Discipline. Departments shape the environment for the faculty, staff, and students comprising the unit. Departmental or disciplinary contexts have been called a "microclimate" because microclimates may represent the larger campus climate or may reflect a different image altogether (Vaccaro, 2012). Nexus studies focusing on the combination of LGBTQ people and ideas with literature related to science, technology, engineering, and math (STEM) point out a less than positive experience for LGBTQ faculty and students (Billimoria & Stewart, 2009; Patridge, Bartholomy, & Rankin, 2014). Other studies have pointed to the social sciences and the humanities as being more "welcoming" to LGBTQ people (Linley, Renn, & Woodford, 2014; Brown, Clarke, Gortmaker, & Robinson-Keilig, 2004). These differences are saliently captured in Brown et al.'s (2004) campus climate study of disciplinary contexts when the authors stated that "soft sciences" are likely a "more fruitful starting place for seeking faculty allies than those in the hard sciences" (p. 20). In a study of the academic climate for gay and lesbian science and engineering faculty, Bilimoria and Stewart (2009) posited that "broadly held tenets of the scientific method (for example, positivism, objectivity, rationality)" and general lack of awareness about sexuality and gender identity suggested that "LGBT issues might be unusually unlikely to seem important to [cisgender] heterosexual science and engineering faculty" (p. 87). LGBTQ STEM undergraduate and graduate students in a different study (Linley, Renn, & Woodford, 2014) reported some positive interactions with their STEM faculty, though students only disclosed their LGBTQ identities to faculty when they deemed it necessary. For example, several trans∗ students discussed disclosing their identities to faculty by requesting faculty use students' preferred names and gender pronouns (Linley et al., 2014).

Research about LGBTQ STEM students and faculty points to the influence of the prevailing STEM ontology on LGBTQ individuals' experiences in STEM curricular contexts. In short, positivism and objectivity foster an environment in which LGBTQ issues and people are perceived as irrelevant. This external influence results in curricular contexts in which LGBTQ students do not bring their full selves. In contrast, some curricular contexts are perceived as open and affirming environments for LGBTQ students as a result of external disciplinary influence. For example, the National Association of Social Workers' (2014) "Code of Ethics" explicitly calls for social workers to develop knowledge, skills, and awareness about diversity and oppression, including sex, gender identity or expression, and sexual orientation. Given the commitment to multicultural competency in this national organization, one might expect to find positive climates for LGBTQ people and topics in social work academic programs. That was the case in one study of master of social work students, in which participants reported low homophobia and overall positive attitudes about LGBT people (Logie, Bridge, & Bridge, 2007). As such, the curricular contexts for social work majors may be positive spaces where LGBTQ students can bring their full selves. Nevertheless, internal influences also shape the ways in which curricular contexts are experienced. We turn now to those internal influences, both institutional and unit level.

Institutional Influences on LGBTQ Curricular Contexts

Curricular contexts are heavily influenced by institutional features (Lattuca & Stark, 2009). In this section, we explore literature about four institutional influences on LGBTQ curricular contexts: mission, climate, policies, and resources.

Mission.   An institution's mission is a statement about the organization's vision for itself, communicating purpose and values to both internal and external audiences (Lattuca & Stark, 2009; Morphew & Hartley, 2006). At some institutions, the mission is diffuse and points to a variety of commitments that may or may not include a commitment to an inclusive, supportive campus for LGBTQ individuals. At other institutions, the mission dictates decisions and establishes culture. Some religiously affiliated institutions are considered mission-driven. In one study of the campus culture for LGB students at a Catholic college, Love (1998) found that Catholicism "anchored" the college (p. 310). Participants perceived that most of their campus community members rationalized their negative beliefs and fears about LGB people in Catholic tradition and dogma (Love, 1998). Because the college is Catholic in nature, and community members largely held the belief that the Catholic church finds "homosexuality" reprehensible, homophobic students, staff, and faculty felt vindicated in holding fast to their beliefs.

Campus Climate.   Students' academic and social integration are influenced by campus climate (Hurtado, Milem, Clayton-Pedersen, & Allen, 1999; Kuh, 1995). LGBTQ students pay attention to campus climate before they even enroll in college. LGBTQ students in one study (Burleson, 2010) reported that their perceptions of a college's "gay-friendliness" mattered in their college choice process. Black gay males in another study specifically looked for college campuses at which they could "come out" and "live out" (Strayhorn, Blakewood, & DeVita, 2008, p. 98). Squire and Mobley (2014) found that Black gay males' most salient identity influenced their decision, with those strongly identifying with their Black identity attending a historically Black college or university and those either strongly identifying with their sexual identity or not strongly identifying with either identity attending a predominantly White institution. For all participants in that study, multiple facets of campus climate (in other words, institutional history, culture, and diversity) influenced participants' college choices (Squire & Mobley, 2014).

Although many LGBTQ students make choices based on precollege perceptions of climate, findings from climate studies of 4-year (Rankin, 2005; Rankin et al., 2010) and 2-year (Garvey, Taylor, & Rankin, 2014) institutions suggested that campus climates are generally negative spaces for LGBTQ students. College campuses are often mired in experiences of harassment, intimidation, and hostility (Bieschke, Eberz, & Wilson, 2000; Brown et al., 2004; Rankin et al., 2010). In synthesizing past studies of homophobia on campus, Schueler, Hoffman, and Peterson (2009) claimed, "[c]ollege and university campuses continue to be chilly climates at best and places of violence at worst for LGBTQ students" (p. 64). According to Arum and Roksa (2011), negative spaces have adverse effects on student learning. It follows from LGBTQ campus climate studies that LGBTQ students face challenging curricular contexts as a result of negative campus climate.

Campus Policies.   Policies, as reflections of campus values and climate (Dirks, 2011; Iverson, 2007), are a mechanism for institutions to communicate their norms and values (Pitcher, Camacho, Renn, & Woodford, 2014). LGBTQ students in Pitcher et al.'s (2014) study reported nondiscrimination policies that include sexual orientation and gender identity and expression as symbolic of support. Although no participants used their institution's nondiscrimination policy to report bias or seek redress for discrimination, existence of the policy resulted in students feeling supported on campus.

Campus Resources.   Resources specific to LGBTQ students provide safe spaces on campuses where the climate might not be welcoming. In some other chapters in this sourcebook, authors explore LGBTQ resources in depth. Here, we discuss opportunities for ally development (Draughn, Elkins, & Roy, 2002; Woodford, Kolb, Durocher-Radeka, & Javier, 2014) as they influence students' curricular contexts. Commonly referred to as Safe Zone programs, ally development initiatives typically prepare individuals on campus (faculty, staff, students) to provide support to LGBTQ individuals (Draughn et al., 2002; Woodford et al., 2014). Those who complete Safe Zone training display some type of placard to visually indicate they are a "safe" person with whom to talk about LGBTQ issues (Draughn et al., 2002). Although LGBTQ students' curricular environments are positively influenced by faculty and staff who display Safe Zone signs on an individual level, a limitation of these programs is their tendency to ignore systemic oppression and heteronormative and genderist educational environments (Draughn et al., 2002; Woodford et al., 2014).

Unit-Level Influences on LGBTQ Curricular Contexts

Lattuca and Stark (2009) identified leadership, program mission, discipline, faculty, and students as unit-level influences. Each internal influence is not independent; instead, these influences commingle and overlap. For example, institutional leadership directs the trajectory of the university and influences departmental mission. Additionally, departments do not exist independent from the faculty, staff, and students. This section examines two of the largest influences (faculty/staff and students) as discrete microsystems within Bronfenbrenner's (1993) ecological framework.

Faculty/Staff.   Faculty hold a unique position to influence more positive curricular contexts for LGBTQ students through faculty research, teaching, and service. At many institutions, research is the central component of a faculty member's employment. The creation and dissemination of new knowledge are fundamental to advancing one's scholarly career. Faculty often invite undergraduate students to become involved in their research. Scholars studying students participating in faculty research have acknowledged its benefits and impact on learning, persistence, and graduate enrollment (Kilgo, Ezell Sheets, & Pascarella, 2015; Pascarella & Terenzini, 2005). Despite the positive benefits that undergraduate students may receive from participating in faculty research, many faculty members, especially faculty of color, conducting scholarship on or related to their specific self-identity may feel devalued within the academy (Turner, Gonzalez, & Wood, 2008). The same is true for LGBTQ academics. LGBTQ faculty whose scholarship is informed by queer theory may encounter a hostile departmental environment (Taylor & Raeburn, 1995; Vaccaro, 2012;). Students explore their developing identities throughout all of their collegiate contexts, including curricular, and environments where LGBTQ scholarship is devalued may make it difficult to explore one's full identity.

Teaching encompasses a number of roles such as advising students, designing courses, and facilitating classroom environments. Positive interactions with faculty and staff promote positive educational outcomes (Garvey & Inkelas, 2012; Kuh, Kinzie, Schuh, & Whitt, 2005; Pascarella & Terenzini, 2005). A number of studies have explored student satisfaction with faculty interactions, but only two studies explored queer identified student satisfaction with faculty interactions (Garvey & Inkelas, 2012; Sweet, 1996). Garvey and Inkelas (2012) found LGB students were more satisfied with faculty interactions than their straight peers. Few studies have examined how gender nonconforming or trans∗ students feel supported by faculty. Rankin and colleagues (2010) found that 42% of LGBTQ students identified the classroom as the locus of harassment. Faculty have a responsibility to act in the best interest of students and can affirm and support minoritized∗ students by reflecting salient identities in the curriculum (Garvey & Rankin, 2015; Renn, 2000), facilitating students through discourse while avoiding the alienation of LGBTQ students (for example, debunking "antigay rhetoric" [Vaccaro, 2012]), curtailing genderist and heterosexist remarks, and fostering an inclusive learning environment (Linley et al., in press).

Service responsibilities for LGBTQ faculty are not dissimilar to that of other minoritized faculty groups. Tokenization of LGBTQ people becomes commonplace for participation in institutional committees to represent "diversity" (Messinger, 2011). An important, but unrewarded function of LGBTQ faculty service is simply being "out." In a number of studies, students have discussed the importance of having an "out" faculty member or someone who can show support for a student's research interests (Linley et al., in press; Vaccaro, 2012;). Being there for LGBTQ students is particularly challenging for faculty when campus and/or departmental climates promote hostility, feelings of invisibility, and pressure to conceal one's sexual orientation (Bilimoria & Stewart, 2009) or gender identity. This point is exemplified in Patridge and colleagues' (2014) study of climates for LGBTQ faculty in STEM disciplines, in which only 31 of 279 participants were "out." Despite these low numbers, "out" faculty can be a source of support or role model to LGBTQ students (Hylton, 2005; Linley et al., in press; Vaccaro, 2012).

Students.   The largest group with internal influence is student peers. Astin (1993) describes student peers as the "single most potent source of influence on growth and development during the college years" (p. 398). Like faculty, student peers have the ability to enhance or detract from an LGBTQ student perspective (Nguyen et al., 2014). From a positive perspective, peers can support each other inside and outside of the classroom through the formation of academic study groups or social clubs to support academic and social integration (Dennis, Phinney, & Chuateco, 2005). However, one of the primary ways that student peers contribute negatively to curricular contexts is through the use of heterosexist or genderist remarks like "that's so gay," which often describes something "stupid, weird or undesirable" but may be a perceived or intentional microaggression among students with differing sexual orientations (Woodford, Howell, Silverchanz, & Yu, 2012, p. 429). Students experiencing these microaggressions resulting from overt heterosexism often have worse mental health outcomes (Burn, 2010) and refrain from disclosing their sexual identity (Rankin, 2005). Stemming from an overly cisgenderist environment, trans∗ students have reported increased experiences of isolation and segregation resulting from "cisgender people's discomfort around gender variance through transgender 'accommodation'" (Dirks, 2011, p. 142). Students who negatively influence educational experiences run the risk of alienating a student and lessening their sense of belonging (Strayhorn, 2012). A lack of inclusion diminishes a student's sense of belonging in the classroom and may exacerbate or reduce the loneliness that many LGBTQ college students experience (Martin & D'Augelli, 2003).

For some students, the collegiate environment is a place where students from less diverse backgrounds may first encounter a student with a different social identity than their own. The classroom can be a site of inquiry to learn about differing gender identities and sexual orientations (Garvey & Rankin, 2015). Peers can reduce the feelings of alienation and silence that many LGBTQ students feel in the classroom setting. Student peers on college campuses also create "safety nets" (Sarason, Sarason, & Pierce, 1990) and support mechanisms for their fellow classmates to explore proximal and distal elements of the collegiate environment (Dennis et al., 2005).

Creating Positive Curricular Contexts for LGBTQ College Students

At the core of the Person, Process, Context, and Time model (Bronfenbrenner, 1993) resides the individual student. In this chapter we have demonstrated that LGBTQ students are not participating in higher education under a "post-LGBTQ" society and despite higher education's liberal leanings, campus environments skew negatively for LGBTQ students. This begs the question of how the curricular context can support LGBTQ students. Existing research about the sociocultural influences on curricular contexts points us to the following suggestions for practice.

First, it is essential to understand that LGBTQ students' curricular experiences are happening in concomitance with all of their other microsystems, and are influenced by sociocultural forces in their meso-, exo-, and macrosystems. "There is always an interplay between the psychological characteristics of the person and of a specific environment; the one cannot be defined without reference to the other" (Bronfenbrenner, 1989, p. 225). Faculty play an important role in the curricular context and have a responsibility to cultivate and use classroom spaces to positively support students in their learning (Nguyen & Larson, 2015). The curricular context is where many students have interactions with faculty and with each other. Faculty often design the framework for a course, yet students can drive the conversation. Faculty and students together should incorporate contemporary issues into the classroom as it is likely not all students will be on one side of the debate. Engaging in curricular debates may make students and faculty alike feel uncomfortable, but these moments present the opportunity to create dissonance that can foster critical thinking and analytical reasoning skills (Mezirow, 1997).

Second, promoting faculty participation in programs such as Safe Zone is important to fostering a sense of belonging among LGBTQ students. These programs can equip faculty with skills for promoting inclusion, reducing discrimination, and engaging classroom audiences. Students often look to faculty members for guidance, and they should not feel unwelcomed in the classroom or during office hours. Participating in these trainings and adhering stickers or plaques to doors will make LGBTQ students less hesitant about following up with faculty members.

NEW DIRECTIONS FOR STUDENT SERVICES • DOI: 10.1002/ss

Finally, we suggest further interrogation of classroom climates for those marginalized in the LGBTQ community, specifically gender noncomforming and trans∗ students, and queer students of color. These important identity groups are often forgotten because the LGBTQ community receives monolithic treatment, yet these students remain absent from the normative narrative of LGBTQ people on campus. To promote this inclusion, we call upon several microsystems to assist in this developmental process. We encourage LGBTQ centers to advocate for curricular inclusion for trans∗ students and for queer people of color. We encourage Safe Zone programs and faculty development initiatives to include information about intersectionality (Crenshaw, 1991) and multiple dimensions of identity (Abes, Jones, & McEwen, 2007).

Faculty development professionals might also promote strategies for faculty and staff to normalize the use of preferred names and gender pronouns (Linley et al., in press).

Conclusion

"Development is an evolving function of person-environment interaction" (Bronfenbrenner, 1989, p. 10), and it is impossible to understand the person without evaluating the environment. Students' curricular contexts are in relationship with sociocultural internal and external forces. In this chapter, we have elucidated ways that LGBTQ curricular contexts are influenced by some of these forces. Our suggestions flow directly from these influences, and in practice, may help create positive curricular contexts for LGBTQ college students.

∗In this volume, we follow the increasingly common practice of an interdisciplinary community of scholars (such as Benitez, 2010; Chase, Dowd, Pazich, & Bensimon, 2014; Gillborn, 2005; Godard, Mukjerjee, & Mukherjee, 2006; Patton, Harper, & Harris, 2015) to use the term *minoritized* as we discuss those whose sexuality and gender have been consigned to lower status, visibility, and power.

References

Abes, E. S., Jones, S. R., & McEwen, M. K. (2007). Reconceptualizing the model of multiple dimensions of identity: The role of meaning-making capacity in the construction of multiple identities. *Journal of College Student Development*, 48(1), 1–22.

Arum, R., & Roksa, J. (2011). *Academically adrift: Limited learning on college campuses*. Chicago, IL: University of Chicago.

Astin, A. W. (1993). *What matters in college?: Four critical years revisited*. San Francisco, CA: Jossey-Bass.

Benitez, M. (2010). Resituating culture centers within a social justice framework: Is there room for examining whiteness? In L. Patton (Ed.), *Culture centers in higher education: Perspectives on identity, theory, and practice* (pp. 119–136). Sterling, VA: Stylus.

Bieschke, K. J., Eberz, A. B., & Wilson, D. (2000). Empirical investigations of lesbian, gay, and bisexual college students. In V. A. Wall & N. J. Evans (Eds.), *Toward acceptance: Sexual orientation issues on campus* (pp. 29–58). Lanham, MD: University Press of America.

Bilimoria, D., & Stewart, A. J. (2009). "Don't ask, don't tell": The academic climate for lesbian, gay, bisexual, and transgender faculty in science and engineering. *NWSA Journal, 21*(2), 85–103.

Bilodeau, B. (2009). *Genderism: Transgender students, binary systems, and higher education.* Saarbru-cken, Germany: VDM Verlag Dr. Müller.

Bronfenbrenner, U. (1989). Ecological systems theory. In R. Vasta (Ed.), *Six theories of development* (pp. 187–249). Greenwich, CT: JAI Press.

Bronfenbrenner, U. (1993). The ecology of cognitive development: Research models and fugitive findings. In R. H. Wozniak & K. W. Fischer (Eds.), *Development in context: Acting and thinking in specific environments* (pp. 3–44). Hillsdale, NJ: Erlbaum.

Brown, R. D., Clarke, B., Gortmaker, V., & Robinson-Keilig, R. (2004). Assessing the campus climate for gay, lesbian, bisexual, and transgender (GLBT) students using a multiple perspectives approach. *Journal of College Student Development, 45*(1), 8–26.

Burleson, D. A. (2010). Sexual orientation and college choice: Considering campus climate. *About Campus, 14*(6), 9–14.

Burn, S. M. (2010). Heterosexuals' use of "fag" and "queer" to deride one another: A contributor to heterosexism and stigma. *Journal of Homosexuality, 40*, 1–11.

Chase, M. M., Dowd, A. C., Pazich, L. B., & Bensimon, E. M. (2014). Transfer equity for "minoritized" students: A critical policy analysis of seven states. *Educational Policy, 28*(5), 669–717.

Crenshaw, K. (1991). Mapping the margins: Intersectionality, identity politics, and violence against women of color. *Stanford Law Review*, 1241–1299.

Dennis, J. M., Phinney, J. S., and Chuateco, L. I. (2005). The role of motivation, parental support, and peer support in the academic success of ethnic minority first generation college students. *Journal of College Student Development, 46*, 223–236.

Dirks, D. A. (2011). *Transgender people on university campuses: A policy discourse analysis.* Unpublished doctoral dissertation.

Draughn, T., Elkins, B., & Roy, R. (2002). Allies in the struggle: Eradicating homophobia and heterosexism on campus. *Journal of Lesbian Studies, 6*(3–4), 9–20.

Garvey, J. C., & Inkelas, K. K. (2012). Exploring relationships between sexual orientation and satisfaction with faculty and staff interactions. *Journal of Homosexuality, 59*(8), 1167–1190.

Garvey, J. C., & Rankin, S. R. (2015). Making the grade? Classroom climate for LGBTQ students across gender conformity. *Journal of Student Affairs Research and Practice, 52*(2), 190–203.

Garvey, J. C., Taylor, J. L., & Rankin, S. R. (2014). An examination of campus climate for LGBTQ community college students. *Community College Journal of Research and Practice*, 1–15.

Ghaziani, A. (2011). Post-gay collective identity construction. *Social Problems, 58*(1), 99–125.

Gillborn, D. (2005). Education policy as an act of white supremacy: Whiteness, critical race theory and education reform. *Journal of Education Policy, 20*(4), 485–505.

Godard, B. J., Mukjerjee, A. P., & Mukherjee, A. (2006). Translating minoritized cultures: Issues of caste, class and gender. *Postcolonial Text, 2*(3), 1–23.

Hatzenbuehler, M. L. (2009). How does sexual minority stigma "get under the skin"? A psychological mediation framework. *Psychological bulletin, 135*(5), 707–730.

Human Rights Campaign (2014). *Support the Equality Act.* Retrieved from http://www.hrc.org/campaigns/support-the-equality-act.

Hurtado, S., Milem, J. F., Clayton-Pedersen, A. R., & Allen, W. R. (1999). Enacting diverse learning environments: Improving the campus climate for racial/ethnic diversity. [*ASHE/ERIC Higher Education Report, 26*(8)]. San Francisco, CA: Jossey-Bass.

Hylton, M. E. (2005). Heteronormativity and the experiences of lesbian and bisexual women as social work students. *Journal of Social Work Education, 41*(1), 67–82.

Iverson, S. V. (2007). Camouflaging power and privilege: A critical race analysis of university diversity policies. *Educational Administration Quarterly, 43*(5), 586–611.

Kilgo, C. A., Ezell Sheets, J. K., & Pascarella, E. T. (2015). The link between high-impact practices and student learning: Some longitudinal evidence. *Higher Education, 69*(4), 509–525.

Kuh, G. D. (1995). The other curriculum: Out-of-class experiences associated with student learning and personal development. *Journal of Higher Education, 66*(2), 123–155.

Kuh, G. D., Kinzie, J., Schuh, J. H., & Whitt, E. J. (2005, 2010). *Student success in college: Creating conditions that matter.* San Francisco, CA: Jossey-Bass.

LaSala, M. C., Jenkins, D. A., Wheeler, D. P., & Fredriksen-Goldsen, K. (2008). LGBT faculty, research, and researchers: Risks and rewards. *Journal of Gay & Lesbian Social Services, 20*(3), 253–267.

Lattuca, L. R., & Stark, J. (2009). *Shaping the college curriculum: Academic plans in action* (2nd ed.). San Francisco, CA: Jossey-Bass.

Linley, J. L., Nguyen, D. J., Brazelton, G. B., Becker, B., Renn, K. A. & Woodford, M. (in press). Faculty as sources of support to LGBTQ college students. *College Teaching.*

Linley, J. L., Renn, K. A., & Woodford, M. (2014, April). *Examining the academic microsystems of successful LGBT STEM majors.* Paper presented at the annual meeting of the American Educational Research Association, Philadelphia, PA.

Logie, C., Bridge, T. J., & Bridge, P. D. (2007). Evaluating the phobias, attitudes, and cultural competence of master of social work students toward the LGBT populations. *Journal of Homosexuality, 53*(4), 201–221.

Love, P. G. (1998). Cultural barriers facing lesbian, gay, and bisexual students at a Catholic college. *Journal of Higher Education, 69*(3), 298–323.

Martin, J. I., & D'Augelli, A. R. (2003). How lonely are gay and lesbian youth? *Psychological Reports, 93*, 486.

Messinger, L. (2011). A qualitative analysis of faculty advocacy on LGBT issues on campus. *Journal of Homosexuality, 58*(9), 1281–1305

Mezirow, J. (1997). Transformative learning: Theory to practice. In P. Cranton (Ed.), *New Directions for Adult and Continuing Education: No. 74. Transformative learning in action: Insights from practice* (pp. 5–12). San Francisco, CA: Jossey-Bass.

Morphew, C. C., & Hartley, M. (2006). Mission statements: A thematic analysis of rhetoric across institutional type. *Journal of Higher Education, 77*(3), 456–471.

National Association of Social Workers. (2014). *Code of ethics.* Retrieved from http://www.naswdc.org/pubs/code/code.asp.

National Coalition of Anti-Violence Programs. (2012). *Hate violence against lesbian, gay, bisexual, transgender, queer, and HIV-affected communities in the United States in 2011.* New York, NY: Author.

Ng, E. (2013), A "post-gay" era? Media gaystreaming, homonormativity, and the politics of LGBT integration. *Communication, Culture & Critique, 6*, 258–283. doi: 10.1111/cccr.12013

Nguyen, D. J., Gonyo, C., Brazelton, G. B., Secrist, S., Long, L. D., Renn, K. A., & Woodford, M. (2014, November). *Peers as sources of support to LGBTQ college students.* Paper presented at the annual meeting of the Association for the Study of Higher Education. Washington, DC.

Nguyen, D. J., & Larson, J. B. (2015). Don't forget about the body: Exploring the curricular possibilities of embodied pedagogy. *Innovative Higher Education, 40*(4), 1–14. http://www.ostem.org/about

Pascarella, E. T., & Terenzini, P. T. (2005). *How college affects students* (Vol. 2). San Francisco, CA: Jossey-Bass.

Patridge, E. V., Barthelemy, R. S., & Rankin, S. R. (2014). Factors impacting the academic climate for LGBQ STEM faculty. *Journal of Women and Minorities in Science and Engineering, 20*(1), 75–98.

Patton, L. D., Harper, S. R., & Harris, J. (2015). Using critical race theory to (re)interpret widely studied topics related to U.S. higher education. In A. M. Martinez-Alemán, B. Pusser, & E. M. Bensimon (Eds.), *Critical approaches to the study of higher education: A practical introduction* (pp. 193–219). Baltimore, MD: Johns Hopkins University.

Pitcher, E., Camacho, T., Renn, K. A., & Woodford, M. (2014, November). *Affirming policies, programs, and supportive services: Understanding organizational support for LGBTQ+ college student success.* Paper presented at the annual meeting of the Association for the Study of Higher Education, Washington, DC.

Rankin, S. R. (2005). Campus climates for sexual minorities. In R. Sanlo (Ed.), *New Directions for Student Services: No. 111. Gender identity and sexual orientation: Research, policy, and personal perspectives* (pp.17–23). San Francisco, CA: Jossey-Bass.

Rankin, S., Weber, G., Blumenfeld, W., & Frazer, S. (2010). *2010 state of higher education for lesbian, gay, bisexual & transgender people.* Charlotte, NC: Campus Pride.

Renn, K. A. (2000). Including all voices in the classroom: Teaching lesbian, gay, and bisexual students. *College Teaching, 48,* 129–135.

Sarason, I. G., Sarason, B. R., & Pierce, G. R. (1990). Social support: The search for theory. *Journal of Social & Clinical Psychology, 9,* 133–147.

Schueler, L. H., Hoffman, J. A., & Peterson, E. (2009). Fostering safe, engaging campuses for lesbian, gay, bisexual, transgender, and questioning students. In S. R. Harper & S. J. Quaye (Eds.), *Student engagement in higher education: Theoretical perspectives and practical approaches for diverse populations* (pp. 61–79). New York: Routledge.

sollender, j. (2011, August 12). Are we entering a post-gay era? *Rage Monthly.* Retrieved from http://www.ragemonthly.com/2011/08/12/are-we-entering-a-post-gay-era-2/.

Squire, D. D., & Mobley, S. D. (2014). Negotiating race and sexual orientation in the college choice process of black gay males. *Urban Review,* 1–26.

Strayhorn, T. L. (2012). *College students' sense of belonging: A key to educational success for all students.* New York, NY: Routledge.

Strayhorn, T. L., Blakewood, A. M., & DeVita, J. M. (2008). Factors affecting the college choice of African American gay male undergraduates: Implications for retention. *NASAP Journal, 11*(1), 88–108.

Sweet, M. J. (1996). Counseling satisfaction of gay, lesbian, and bisexual college students. *Journal of Gay & Lesbian Social Services, 4,* 35–49.

Taylor, V., & Raeburn, N. C. (1995). Identity politics as high-risk activism: Career consequences for lesbian, gay, and bisexual sociologists. *Social Problems, 42,* 252–273.

Tinto, V. (1987). *Leaving college: Rethinking the causes and cures of student attrition* (1st ed.). Chicago, IL: University of Chicago.

Tinto, V. (1993). *Leaving college: Rethinking the causes and cures of student attrition* (2nd ed.). Chicago, IL: University of Chicago.

Tompkins, A. (2014). Asterisk. *Transgender Studies Quarterly, 1*(1–2), 26–27.

Turner, C. S. V., Gonzales, J. C., & Wood, J. L. (2008). Faculty of color in academe: What 20 years of literature tells us. *Journal of Diversity in Higher Education, 1,* 39–168.

Vaccaro, A. (2012). Campus microclimates for LGBT faculty, staff, and students: An exploration of the intersections of social identity and campus roles. *Journal of Student Affairs Research and Practice, 49*(4), 429–446.

Woodford, M. R., Howell, M. L., Silverschanz, P., & Yu, L. (2012). "That's so gay!" Examining the covariates of hearing this expression among gay, lesbian, and bisexual college students. *Journal of American College Health, 60*(6), 429–434.

Woodford, M. R., Kolb, C. L., Durocher-Radeka, G., & Javier, G. (2014). Lesbian, gay, bisexual, and transgender ally training programs on campus: current variations and future directions. *Journal of College Student Development, 55*(3), 317–322.

Youth Suicide Prevention Program. (2014). *Statistics about youth suicide.* Retrieved from http://www.yspp.org/about_suicide/statistics.htm.

JODI L. LINLEY is visiting instructor and program coordinator of the Higher Education and Student Affairs Program at The University of Iowa.

DAVID J. NGUYEN is a doctoral candidate in the Higher, Adult, and Lifelong Education program at Michigan State University.

NEW DIRECTIONS FOR STUDENT SERVICES • DOI: 10.1002/ss

4

In this chapter, the authors consider issues of LGBTQA+ representation and visibility across cocurricular departments in U.S. colleges and universities. There is also a particular focus on identity-based centers and their role in facilitating LGBTQA+ inclusion.

Cocurricular and Campus Contexts

Debra Bazarsky, Leslie K. Morrow, Gabriel C. Javier

As discussed in previous chapters, the meaning of lesbian, gay, bisexual, transgender, queer, asexual or some other minoritized sexual orientations and gender identities (LGBTQA+[1]) continues to change across time and context. These changes occur on and off campus, at the same time that students engage in activities to explore and enact with their genders and sexualities. Historical and recent advances in the sociopolitical climate have greatly influenced the ways colleges and universities support and engage LGBTQA+ students inside and outside the classroom. In Chapter Three, Jodi Linley and David Nguyen addressed academic contexts for LGBTQA+ students, and in this chapter we address cocurricular contexts and campus environment.

In this chapter, we explore the representation and visibility of LGBTQA+ issues across cocurricular departments in higher education. We describe the historical and contemporary contexts for LGBTQA+ student life, including challenges to higher education and new ways in which students claim their sexual and gender identities. The ways students engage within campus contexts, as well as opportunities and challenges for LGBTQA+-inclusive campus climates, across different units are also considered. We make suggestions for student affairs and auxiliary services to become truly inclusive of LGBTQA+ identities. Finally, we discuss identity-based centers as vehicles and facilitators of campus LGBTQA+ work. Note that we follow the increasingly common practice of an interdisciplinary community of scholars (such as Benitez, 2010; Chase, Dowd, Pazich, & Bensimon, 2014; Gillborn, 2005; Godard, Mukjerjee, & Mukherjee, 2006; Patton, Harper, & Harris, 2015) to use the term *minoritized* as we discuss those whose sexuality and gender have been consigned to lower status, visibility, and power.

---

[1] To ensure the inclusion of students who identify as asexual, or "ace," we and other LGBT campus resource professionals increasingly use the abbreviation LGBTQA+. The plus symbol gives deference to any identities beyond or between the enumerated letters, and/or outside binary conceptions of gender and sexual identities.

NEW DIRECTIONS FOR STUDENT SERVICES, no. 152, Winter 2015 © 2015 Wiley Periodicals, Inc.
Published online in Wiley Online Library (wileyonlinelibrary.com) • DOI: 10.1002/ss.20145

Historical Context

Many institutions of higher education have come a long way in support-ing LGBTQA+ students, but this was not the case for most of the last century. LGBTQA+ students, staff, faculty, and graduates encountered in-stitutionalized and personally directed homophobia, biphobia, and trans-phobia (Dilley, 2002; Marine, 2011). Before formal institutional support existed in, for example, student organizations, campus counseling centers, and LGBTQA+ campus resource centers, and while most employees re-mained closeted, students led the way in attempting to transform colleges and universities. Students began to organize officially in the late 1960s and early 1970s, just as the "gay" political movement stepped into the spot-light (Marine, 2011). Throughout the 1970s and 1980s more colleges and universities established organizations, which were initiated by students for support and community. Over time these organizations began to change institutional climates (Marine, 2011; Miller, 1995).

The first LGBTQA+ office was founded at the University of Michigan in 1971. Although a few other campuses founded centers in the 1970s and 1980s, it was not until the 1990s and 2000s that many more campuses in-stitutionalized support in a more formal and intentional manner (Sanlo, Rankin, & Schoenberg, 2002). In addition, throughout the 1990s and 2000s many student affairs and auxiliary services units (e.g., residence life, student activities, Greek life, counseling and health services, and offices providing services to graduates) explored how they could be a better resource and sup-port for the LGBTQA+ students with whom they worked. At the same time a proliferation of identity development models came out of higher educa-tion, sociology, and psychology research to help professionals better under-stand the identity and experiences of LGBTQA+ members of the campus community (see Bilodeau & Renn, 2005).

The struggle to establish visibility and support for members of the LGBTQA+ community often came at the expense of public shaming, job loss, incarceration, and in some cases, violence and death (Marine, 2011; Vaid, 1995). Today, those circumstances still exist for many people from minoritized gender and sexual identity groups, especially in some international contexts. For most U.S. colleges and universities, the work toward full LGBTQA+ inclusion must evolve to reflect the changing demographics and social contexts of contemporary campus communities. Traditional LGBTQA+ advocacy that focused on raising visibility and challenging stigma has expanded to include nuanced work across a number of new functional and infrastructure areas (e.g., technological responses to "preferred" name processes,[2] medical insurance inclusions and exclusions,

---

[2]We use quotes around "preferred" because for trans* students, this name is not a prefer-ence but simply their name. However, for a variety of reasons (e.g., legal, visa, financial, familial), students are unable to change their legal name. Many colleges and universities name these procedures "preferred name policies."

NEW DIRECTIONS FOR STUDENT SERVICES • DOI: 10.1002/ss

and construction and design standards). As institutions of higher learning adjust to a wider scope of LGBTQA+ support and services, the need continues for student services' and auxiliary services' offices, staff and faculty across campus, and institutions in the larger context to raise their own cultural capacity and competency to support LGBTQA+ students, staff, faculty, and alumni.

Sociopolitical Context for LGBTQA+ Students in Higher Education

Just as civil rights for individuals with minoritized sexual or gender identities have evolved over time, conditions for LGBTQA+ students on college campuses have improved substantially since the era when they were expelled, treated as psychologically ill, and routinely harassed. LGBTQA+ student activists have played important roles in bringing about change in higher education and they have much to celebrate. Yet a number of macro-level social and political factors converge to create tensions between the narrative of progress toward social justice and the lived experience of LGBTQA+ people across categories of, for example, race, citizenship, and social class. These tensions amplify in a higher education context that is itself under scrutiny regarding costs and student debt, graduation rates and preparation for careers, and policies related to campus sexual assault and violence.

Substantial advances in the overall sociopolitical context have influenced campus climate for LGBTQA+ people, which in turn calls for changes in higher education practice and theory. With cultural acceptance, supportive laws, and policy changes, young people the United States may experience increased acceptance compared to past generations of LGBTQA+ youth. They have access to media and digital communities that provide myriad models for and ways to think about their LGBTQA+ identities (Craig & McInroy, 2014). Some campuses have sizable trans*[3] communities, and increasingly, more students identify along the asexual spectrum, with some LGBTQA+ offices sponsoring groups and programming (for a discussion of asexual college students, see McAleavey, Castonguay, & Locke, 2011). More students than in previous decades identify as nonmonosexual, pansexual, and fluid, in addition to queer (see Callis, 2014).

In response to changes at all levels of the environment, campus professionals must continually update resources and services; educate colleagues accordingly; and ensure that knowledge, language, resources, program-

---

[3]As explained by T.J. Jourian in his chapter in this volume, "The asterisk at the end of the prefix trans is used to signal broad inclusivity of multiple gender identities beyond just trans men (also referred to as female-to-male or transgender men) or trans women (also referred to as male-to-female or transgender women), such as nonbinary individuals, as well as crossdressers and even gender performers like drag kings and queens (Tompkins, 2014)."

ming, and support remain up to date and evolving to meet the changing nature of all students' identities. They must do so in a higher education context that is itself changing. The majority of all college students take nonlinear paths through college, accumulating credits at two or more institutions (Renn & Reason, 2013); adjunct and other nontenure track faculty teach increasing numbers of student credit hours (Kezar, 2012); and digital technologies have substantially changed teaching, learning, and relating to one another on campus (Bowen, 2015). Neoliberal values cast higher education as a private, rather than public, good and encourage a view of students as consumers in a free market economy that pits institutions against one another for "customers" and resources (see Giroux, 2002).

LGBTQA+ Student Experiences

Although no monolithic experience exists for any category of student, traditional-age lesbian, gay, and bisexual (LGB) students have always known "out" ("out of the closet" or openly known as LGB) characters on television and have likely been aware of out musicians, athletes, and politicians. Many had Gay/Straight Alliances in their high schools, as well as out friends and family members. As noted previously, they have numerous examples of ways to be queer in a diverse community with a growing openness to a wide range of labels and flexibility of identity. Some LGB students have been out since childhood with no memory of being in the metaphorical closet in the same ways it was constructed in the past (Bazarsky & Sanlo, 2011). In what sociologist Steven Seidman called the "post-closet era," there has been a shift away from the "closet," as it was once known, toward a time of self-acceptance, disclosure, and integration of one's identity in social life (Seidman, 2004).

Despite this shift, there are still a large number of students who struggle with coming out, wait until they graduate to come out, or who are unable to be fully out (Herdt, 2013; Peña-Talamantes, 2013; Russon & Schmidt, 2014). Such individuals may be, for example, out at home and closeted at school or out on campus and closeted at work. LGBTQA+ discrimination, harassment, and violence continue to be a major national issue in communities, schools, and colleges (Kosciw, Greytak, Palmer, & Boesen, 2014; Rankin, Weber, Blumenfeld, Frazer, & Pride, 2010), with young trans* women of color most at risk (Ahmed & Jindasurat, 2014). Compared with straight and cisgender[4] peers LGBTQA+ youth continue to have higher rates of homelessness, violent victimization, suicide, self-harming behaviors, sexual health risks, new HIV infections, psychological distress, substance abuse, and other mental and physical health disparities (Johnson

---

[4]Cisgender is used to refer to those persons whose internal gender identity matches social expectations for the biological sex they were designated at birth.

& Amella, 2014; Keuroghlian, Shtasel, & Bassuk, 2014; Liu & Mutanski, 2012).

Although many LGBTQA+ people still face insurmountable struggles, as LGBTQA+ civil rights progress—for example, marriage equality—some students and administrators believe that society has reached full support for LGBTQA+ people. Some out students who perceive this time as a "postgay era" identify increasingly in opposition to LGBTQA+ programs, affiliated groups, and activism on their campus (see Ghaziani, 2011; Swank & Fahs, 2012). Encountering microaggressions and bias often shatter this post-gay lens, and empirical evidence demonstrates that youth in general have not abandoned LGB identities (Russell, Clarke, & Clary, 2009).

Still, students and others who perceive society as postgay may question the relevance and necessity of LGBTQA+ services and support, even as other students cite these resources as critical to academic, personal, and social success (Nguyen et al., 2014). In contrast to students who view society and themselves as postgay, the continued challenges, including frequent invisibility of trans*, nonbinary, and queer lives in policy and practice, contribute to the increased complexity and criticality of these services and supports (Patton, Kortegast, & Javier, 2011).

What does this diversity in perspectives about LGBTQA+ identity and the changing face of LGBTQA+ students mean for higher education professionals in a neoliberal context? Marine and Nicolazzo (2014) suggested that the historical commitment of the field of student affairs to promoting equity and justice stands in contrast to the neoliberal turn in higher education. Even as student affairs educators welcome new expressions of sexual orientation and gender identities, LGBTQA+ students may be pressured—directly or indirectly—to dampen their activism and advocacy efforts in these areas. Changes in students and the context of higher education require changes in the work of professionals in student affairs, auxiliary services, and other parts of the institution that support students in cocurricular contexts.

Changing Campus Contexts

Despite progress that is evident in institutional policy changes, programs, and curriculum, more intentional, collaborative, and intersectional work needs to occur in all facets of the institution to provide fully inclusive environments for students of every sexual and gender identity. Even at campuses that repeatedly rate high in serving LGBTQA+ students, anecdotally, students report major issues with homophobia/biphobia/transphobia, hetero/cissexism, being outed by others, and feeling isolated on campus. In addition, campuses struggle with the implementation of new policies and procedures, as well as the assessment and transformation of climate (Brown & Gortmaker, 2009; Vaccaro, 2012). As far as colleges have progressed, more is needed to support LGBTQA+ students.

The continuously changing nature of LGBTQA+ identities, language and terminology, community expectations, and changing customs has implications for higher education professionals (Marine & Nicolazzo, 2014). These changes are especially relevant as they relate to engaging with and supporting student leaders and campus activists, knowing current "best practices" when advocating for LGBTQA+ matters, and engaging with students and the community. We offer three examples that illustrate the changing nature of identity and the ways that higher education professionals who are trying to support students sometimes may help them feel included or alienated. In each, there is evidence of progress and inclusion, along with evidence of exclusion, and microaggressions that contribute to a hostile climate.

Example 1. There is a cultural shift in many cocurricular contexts, to conduct introductions by inviting people to give their chosen name and pronoun (e.g., she, her, hers; they, them, their; ze, hir, hirs). Student groups and residence hall floors might start each meeting with members giving names and pronouns, acknowledging that identities may change over time. But because this practice is inconsistent across campus, LGBTQA+ students then enter spaces where this inclusive practice does not exist and other campus actors misgender them, assuming incorrect pronouns, and using the wrong names. The inconsistency may lead students to mistrust some professionals and the offices in which they work, reducing the chances that the student would reach out to this resource in the future. Misgendering takes place in many forms across campus: Public safety officers handling a room lockout and making the assumption of the gender of the person based on the sound of their voice; a medical provider who knows a student's gender identity and pronouns but regularly— purposefully or accidentally—uses incorrect pronouns about the student in the presence of others; a simple statement like "May I have your attention, ladies" in a sorority meeting.

Example 2. Many campuses offer programs related to promoting wellness and healthy sexual behaviors, which we consider a potentially positive resource. Inclusion of diverse sexual and gender identities in sessions on safer sex, sexual assault, and wellness are especially welcome developments. However, many people wrongly assume that all members of the LGBTQA+ community prioritize their sexuality and/or are sexually active. This assumption builds from a societal assumption that all people are sexual beings and the disproven but persistent, narrow stereotype that LGBTQA+ identity equates to enacting sexual behavior. Orientation, peer health, and other programs that operate from the assumption that all people are sexually active and desire to be sexual alienate many asexual students (Chasin, 2015; McAleavey et al., 2011). Programs that focus heavily on consent and acknowledge a wide range of sexual desire include asexual students more fully.

Example 3. Because LGBTQA+ identities have become commonplace among students on many campuses there are many student leaders who are out but may not identify with the LGBTQA+ campus community (Seidman, 2004). Professionals may—in a show of support—try to connect with students regarding the student's LGBTQ+ identity, only to be pushed away or rebuffed by the student, who chooses to focus on other identities and interests instead of their LGBTQ+ identification.

These three examples offer a window into the growing complexities of LGBTQA+ students' engagement. With identity categories expanding and shifting as some professionals still lack information about these identities, some interactions may lead to students feeling professionals have committed microaggressions or worse. In our observations, some staff trivialize these incidents as examples of excessive "political correctness." However, for LGBTQA+ students, even as the overall campus climate improves, these incidents negatively shape the college experience and illuminate damaging aspects of campus climate (Rankin et al., 2010; Woodford, Howell, Silverschanz, & Yu, 2012). Staff, faculty, and administrators play a substantial role as colleges and universities become more diverse and as institutions try to shift campus climates in profound ways. In the next section, we explore ways in which inclusion efforts in functional units and overall institutional commitment affect the cocurricular context for LGBTQA+ students.

Growing Institutional Capacity Through Increased Unit Competency

The work of increasing the capacity of an institution to create and maintain an inclusive and affirming campus climate for LGBTQA+ students must include the work of units across campus and the commitment of the institution writ large. Concurrently, although affirming policy may not necessarily positively shift culture, campus culture certainly has little incentive or motivation to change absent such policies (Ahmed, 2012). In short, raising the capacity of an institution toward being more LGBTQA+ inclusive must include enumerated commitments by the larger institution and also the investment of units in being vehicles of these commitments. Here we discuss the ways that both institutions and units can move toward increasing LGBTQA+ inclusion for students.

Across functional units, professionals need to develop a general understanding of the diversity and wide range of experiences of LGBTQA+ people and their needs (Rankin et al, 2010). Particulars of LGBTQA+ inclusion will differ given campus contexts, yet frameworks that centralize a positive cumulative impact on campus climate, alongside the framework of universal design, provide fertile ground for LGBTQA+ inclusion to take root. A few basic tenets here are important to emphasize: the decoupling of notions of gender, sex, and sexual orientation; familiarity in concept and practice of chosen names and pronouns (including nongendered pronouns); awareness of resources for LGBTQA+ students; and visibility and representation of LGBTQA+ lives across the college life cycle. Across units, especially in those that are not explicitly based on social identities (LGBTQA+ or otherwise), inclusive practice that reflects these tenets begins to speak to an institution's commitment to LGBTQA+ students.

Cumulative Impact and Universal Design

There are over 200 LGBTQA+-specific centers and offices on U.S. college campuses and a few in Canada (see www.lgbtcampus.org). Although such a unit can serve as a central point of consultation, contact, and resource provision, it would be inappropriate for a campus, regardless of size, to depend solely on the efforts of that center to raise LGBTQA+ cultural capacity throughout campus. In the same ways that units, departments, and schools share responsibility for fostering inclusive spaces for students of color, international students, and students with disabilities, so too should they share responsibility for creating inclusive spaces for LGBTQA+ students. In this distributed approach, LGBTQA+ students benefit from the cumulative impact of inclusive environments across functional units. This positive cumulative impact, in the form of microaffirmations, becomes a direct response to the negative cumulative impact resulting from repeated microagressions (Rowe, 2008).

A universal design framework can also be an effective complement to considerations of cumulative impact. Adapted from the disability rights movement, universal design—in its conception, application, and use—is collaborative by nature. Universal design hinges on the idea that a particular accommodation is good for many students beyond a population for which the accommodation may be most obvious or requested (Johnson & Fox, 2003). Therefore, it may be effective to frame policy or system changes as having a positive effect beyond those felt by LGBTQA+ communities. Two current examples are chosen or "preferred" name policies and all-gender restroom construction. Chosen or "preferred" names are those used by students that may differ from their legal name. Through the lens of universal design, it is reasonable to conclude that chosen names, although an accommodation employed by students, faculty, and staff across the trans* spectrum, may have positive implications for other populations, such as international students or students and faculty whose legal name is not the one they use in daily life for any number of reasons. Being able to use one's chosen name in an e-mail address and on class rosters, for example, may reduce incidents of misgendering by faculty and others who receive student lists. For trans* students, chosen names systems recognize names that best reflect their chosen and lived identity. There are a range of potential users, and in our observation international students and students who use nicknames are larger user groups of this system than are trans* students.

Providing all-gender or gender-inclusive restrooms is another example of an accommodation that broadens accessibility and has a reach beyond the population of LGBTQA+ students. People who breastfeed or who have young children, those with mobility attendants, and people who require privacy are examples of populations for whom accessible single-stall, gender-inclusive restrooms easily located on campus may be an asset. The fact that trans* and gender-nonconforming people may feel more comfortable and safer in these restrooms is a direct and added benefit.

Baseline Understanding of Gender, Sex, and Sexual Orientation

Functional units across student affairs and other student services should have a baseline understanding of concepts related to sex assigned at birth, gender identity, gender expression, and sexual and romantic orientation. These aspects of self are independent from one other and exist along spectra of experience, as opposed to in binary expressions (see Patton, Renn, Guido, & Quaye, 2016). Being able to conceptualize how these different aspects of self interact with one another serves as the basis for understanding trans* identities and also opens the door for straight-identified, cisgender, and sexual people to reflect on their own experiences of gender and sexuality injustice and prejudice (Case & Meier, 2014; Kelly, 2014). Emerging identities, like those across the asexual ("ace") spectrum or those who identify across nonmonosexual identities, should also be included in professionals' growing understanding of sex, gender, and attraction. Functionally, examples of how this knowledge may lead to change are (a) front desk or greeting policies, whereby clients or students are addressed by the correct name; (b) applications, intake, and information forms and survey questions regarding sex or gender that are expanded to include response options beyond binary male/man and female/woman; and (c) staff training procedures that begin to include practice scenarios that highlight competent and inclusive ways to work with trans* and gender-nonconforming people and students with minoritized sexual identities. Decoupling notions of gender identity, gender expression, sex, and sexual orientation expands capacity to provide inclusive programs and services.

Inclusive Language

We advocate the use of inclusive language to signify, establish, and sometimes create environments with intentionality, rather than politically correct language, which people often use to protect themselves from being perceived as exclusive or unfriendly (Andrews, 1996; Killerman, 2013). Inclusive language, then, becomes a strong but subtle indicator that a system, institution, or group acknowledges and affirms the experiences of people who are not commonly represented by the majority or groups that have access, power, and privilege. Exclusive language can often manifest itself in the form of microinvalidations, a type of microaggression that nullifies the lived experiences of a particular group (Sue et al., 2007). Spoken or written language that assumes an individual's sexual orientation or gender identity is one example of a microinvalidation. As noted earlier, including only binary options for the collection of sex/gender on institutional forms excludes people whose identities are in between or outside a male/man and female/woman construct. Similarly, a form that asks about a student's mother and father invalidates the experience of students whose family models do not include a mother or father in a two-parent, binary, woman-and-man combination.

In contrast, asking students for chosen or "preferred" names and inquiring about the pronouns that they use is a form of interpersonal communication that denotes what Obear (2013) called *distinguishing behavior* on the part of the staff member employing the strategy. The concept of distinguishing behavior communicates the idea of behavior that sets a service provider—especially one with majority or privileged identities—apart from others who are in similar positions of power and who may be less affirming or inclusive (Obear, 2013). Asking a person's chosen or "preferred" name can also help to build affinity between people and to establish positive relationships. Additionally, student services and other offices can enact new interpersonal norms whereby everyone provides their pronouns in use rather than leave that question open to assumptions based on perceived gender (e.g., "Hi my name is Gianna, but I go by Gia, I use she/her/hers pronouns, how about you?"). This practice reinforces the notion that everyone, not only trans* individuals, chooses their pronouns, though many cisgender individuals have never had to consider them a choice; it also reminds cisgender individuals of the privilege that they hold on this issue.

It is important to note that if unit procedure or interpersonal practice includes asking for and collecting a student's chosen name, pronoun-in-use, or both, there is an implicit expectation that professionals will use those identifiers. A microinvalidation can occur if, for example, an advisor asks for an advisee's chosen or "preferred" name but then does not use that name in correspondence or communication. Similarly, any unit practice or procedure that includes the use of chosen or "preferred" names and pronouns-in-use should also address how communities of practice react and respond when staff use an incorrect name or pronoun or otherwise disclose sensitive aspects of a student's identity.

Being a Good Resource

Regardless of the department or unit, staff members in student affairs and auxiliary services serve as campus resources. The nature of the resource ranges from advising on an academic field of study, to constructing a resume, to addressing wellness concerns, and beyond. Being involved in students' lives opens up the potential to be privy to and consultant for their holistic development, often outside the specific resource unit.

The positive and inclusive ways a staff member talks about LGBTQA+ people can indicate for a student whether that staff member is a potential resource. Knowledge of campus and community referrals helps make staff members a strong resource. These referrals may include a connection to a campus LGBTQA+ center, familiarity with affirming counselors on campus, or information about LGBTQA+-affirming places of worship, to name a few. Regardless of whether a staff member has these resources readily available, a willingness to help the student find the appropriate referral communicates active allyship and a willingness to journey with a student instead of handing them off to an unknown outlet.

Representing LGBTQA+ Lives Across the College Life Cycle

It is important for units across functional areas to develop practices that consider how a diversity of students may encounter, interact with, and regard their services. Units that serve from admission through enrollment to postcollege life must filter their services through a rubric of inclusion of LGBTQA+ people. For example, in communication about a program or service, a department should consider ways to indicate that this space is an inclusive one for LGBTQA+ students. Services and programs must be explicit in their inclusion of LGBTQA+ people. Representations of LGBTQA+ lives should move beyond acceptance and tolerance toward celebration and inclusion. Such representations may engender a sense of belonging and acceptance of LGBTQA+ people not only in an individual program but across the campus climate (Woodford & Kulick, 2014). Conducting an audit of all current communications, programs, and services—as well as being mindful in creating new ones—can contribute to positive climate.

Other Unit-Specific Considerations

Whereas the aforementioned tenets serve as effective, overarching starting points, details and specific practices in a variety of units allow staff members to do their work in ways that value the contributions of LGBTQA+ students. When successfully and competently employed, small adjustments to practice alongside big shifts in frameworks mitigate barriers between LGBTQA+ students and their full educational experiences. Interventions exist along continuums that are unit specific, competency based, and broadly applied. We offer three thematic examples that can be modified to speak to specific departmental functions and missions.

- Provide professional development for staff such as ally/safe space training; trans∗ specific workshops; and cultural competency regarding

LGBTQA+ health care, legal issues, policing, and other unit-specific expertise.

- Include programmatic interventions that address biased language in, for example, residence halls, fraternities and sororities, and student leadership and diversity training.
- Create LGBTQA+ services and supports that are unit specific, such as career services advising about LGBTQA+ employment topics, wellness and prevention services that reach out to LGBTQA+ populations, community service focused on LGBTQA+ homelessness, and organizational advising that explores identity-based leadership.
- Develop inclusive procedures and policies, for example inclusion of sexual orientation and gender identity in nondiscrimination policies, electronic records and databases that reflect a student's chosen or "preferred" name and appropriate pronouns, gender-inclusive restrooms as part of institutional design standards, and insurance coverage for trans*-related medical procedures.
- Organize programming that speaks to LGBTQA+ experiences, such as for National LGBTQA+ History Month and National Coming Out Day in October, campus Awareness Weeks and Pride Weeks, and throughout the year.
- Incorporate LGBTQA+ students' multiple identities within annual activities, such as programming with multicultural centers and disability and access offices, orientation, homecoming, admission acceptance days, cultural heritage months and weeks, and religious programming and observances.
- Support LGBTQA+ students and help them carefully consider the effects of disclosure of their identities in contexts outside college, such as when studying abroad, in medical school and law applications, on resumes and in interviews, and to family and friends.
- Design inclusive marketing materials that recruit students with diverse experiences and identities to the institution as prospective students, then as student employees, peer educators, resident advisors, and organization leaders.
- Create physical signs of inclusion, such as gender-inclusive restrooms, locker rooms, athletic facilities, and performance changing facilities, and operationalize inclusion through housing room assignments based on gender identity rather than sex assigned at birth.
- Become familiar with LGBTQA+ topics relevant to your specific unit, for example in study abroad assisting students who need gender-confirming hormones while abroad, in international students offices helping trans* students manage Student and Exchange Visitor Information System regulations, and in conduct offices being aware of the disproportionate impact bias has on LGBTQA+ communities and power dynamics in processes that favor majority populations.

Deep and Broad Impact

These examples are by no means an exhaustive list, and the grounding of general tenets of inclusive practice depends to a great extent on other elements of institutional context. The commitment to creating and sustaining LGBTQA+ affirming environments presents many challenges and opportunities. To some people, it may seem that these interventions and accommodations have a narrow impact, that is, the number of people who access them may be small. However, institutions that employ these practices help create more inclusive environments that meet a diverse range of needs. The presence of inclusive programs, services, and facilities has a considerable impact on students who actively seek them. Considering the concept of gender and sexual orientation inclusion as one of universal design, we have observed on our campuses and others that students across campus, within and beyond the identified LGBTQA+ community, use them and benefit as well.

Collaborating with Professionals in LGBTQA+ Resource Units

The scope and role of LGBTQA+ work within higher education has dramatically expanded since the foundational publication *Our Place on Campus* (Sanlo, Rankin, & Schoenberg, 2002), which described and analyzed what was then an emerging functional unit. There has been a measurable and dramatic increase in the roles of LGBTQA+ centers and the roles of the professionals who staff them, requiring a more intentional collaboration and partnership with student affairs, academic affairs, and auxiliary services. The Consortium of Higher Education LGBT Resource Professionals (www.lgbtcampus.org) provides evidence through self-studies,[5] education, advising, support, and advocacy. These efforts to create and foster campus environments that are safe and inclusive for people of all sexual and gender identities continue to be at the forefront of the work. Examples of the new, broader scope of the consortium's efforts include focusing on wellness (for example, program and support regarding mental health, cognitive disabilities, and healthier living); working with colleagues on recruitment, retention, and degree completion initiatives as central to the unit's mission; keeping LGBTQA+ students engaged, safe, and feeling welcomed as critical components of academic success through a variety of institutional partnerships; shepherding students through Title IX and judicial processes; and helping students address the intersections of multiple, competing, and sometimes conflicting social identities.

Campus models are changing in order to reflect and meet the demands of constituents and to help create a more welcoming campus climate. As

---

[5]The consortium conducts self-studies about the profession (e.g., shifting roles, reporting lines, salaries, resources, and programs), which are unpublished and accessible to members at www.lgbtcampus.org.

stated earlier, it would be inappropriate for institutions to rely solely upon campus LGBTQA+ resource centers to do all of the work geared toward meeting the needs of this very diverse population, but we strongly encourage institutional leaders to understand, acknowledge, and enlist expertise held by staff, faculty, and in some cases, students who staff these centers. The ability to take an intersectional approach and partner with colleagues to respond to the needs of a diverse student, staff, and faculty population (e.g., people of color, people with disabilities, veterans, undocumented students, first-generation students, athletes) is essential. LGBTQA+ campus centers can play a substantial role in improving campus climate and shaping the experience of LGBTQA+ community members.

Collaborating with a variety of campus departments can be an effective way to meet the growing and intersecting needs of students, staff, and faculty. In our observation, when institutional conversations about diversity and social justice occur, they often lack inclusion of LGBTQA+ issues or a focus on multiple identities, which is a challenge many LGBTQA+ resource professionals are trying to negotiate. Reporting to and working among other offices with similar missions, such as other multicultural programs and services units, creates new opportunities for collaboration and fosters these connections. The wider sociopolitical climate has had an indelible impact upon campus climate, and the work of campus resources centers thus far not only achieves the vision first established in 1971 but also reflects the growing and diverse needs of campus populations including graduates. Yet, substantial work remains, and it is time for both reflection and action with regard to partnership and collaboration in order to meet the needs of diverse campus populations.

Conclusion

For colleges to succeed in meeting important institutional goals during this period of social change, it is important to think of the entire LGBTQA+ community, including students, faculty, staff, and graduates. Campuses must be intentional in creating supportive and affirming cocurricular spaces. They should think broadly in attracting inclusion-minded trustees, administrators, faculty, and staff members. They can support LGBTQA+ students and create a climate where they, in all of their multiple, intersecting identities are fully included. Institutions can recruit and educate future leaders across a range of traditional and emerging disciplinary fields. They can reengage LGBTQA+ graduates, and units across campus can intentionally collaborate with campus LGBTQA+ resource centers to advance diversity and inclusion efforts. Administrative departments that keep up with and support the ever growing and expanding LGBTQA+ community will be attractive to the next generation of students, who are more likely to judge institutions on how we respond to the LGBTQA+

needs of today, and these units will reap the benefits of full inclusion of this vibrant and dynamic community.

References

Ahmed, O., & Jindasurat, C. (2014). *Lesbian, gay, bisexual, transgender, queer, and HIV affected hate violence in 2013.* New York, NY: National Coalition of Anti Violence Programs.

Ahmed, S. (2012). *On being included: Racism and diversity in institutional life.* Durham, NC: Duke University Press.

Andrews, E. (1996). Cultural sensitivity and political correctness: The linguistic problem of naming, *American Speech, 71,* 389–404.

Bazarsky, D., & Sanlo, R. (2011). LGBT students and staff: Emerging legal and policy issues. In L. M. Stulberg & S. L. Weinberg (Eds.). *Diversity in American higher education: Toward a more comprehensive approach* (pp. 128–141). New York, NY: Routledge Press.

Benitez, M. (2010). Resituating culture centers within a social justice framework: Is there room for examining whiteness? In L. Patton (Ed.), *Culture centers in higher education: Perspectives on identity, theory, and practice* (pp. 119–136). Sterling, VA: Stylus.

Bilodeau, B. L., & Renn, K. A. (2005). Analysis of LGBT identity development models and implications for practice. In R. L. Sanlo (Ed.), *New Directions for Student Services: No. 111. Gender identity and sexual orientation: Research, policy, and personal* (pp. 25–39). San Francisco, CA: Jossey-Bass.

Bowen, W. G. (2015). *Higher education in the digital age.* Princeton, NJ: Princeton University Press.

Brown, R. D., & Gortmaker, V. J. (2009). Assessing campus climates for lesbian, gay, bisexual and transgender (LGBT) students: Methodological and political issues. *Journal of LGBT Youth, 6,* 416–435.

Callis, A. S. (2014). Bisexual, pansexual, queer: Non-binary identities and the sexual borderlands. *Sexualities, 17,* 63–80.

Case, K., & Meier, S. (2014). Developing allies to transgender and gender nonconforming youth: Training for counselors and educators. *Journal of LGBT Youth, 11*(1), 62–82.

Chase, M. M., Dowd, A. C., Pazich, L. B., & Bensimon, E. M. (2014). Transfer equity for "minoritized" students: A critical policy analysis of seven states. *Educational Policy, 28*(5), 669–717.

Chasin, C. J. (2015). Making sense in and of the asexual community: Navigating relationships and identities in a context of resistance. *Journal of Community & Applied Social Psychology, 25,* 167–180.

Craig, S. L., & McInroy, L. (2014). You can form a part of yourself online: The influence of new media on identity development and coming out for LGBTQ youth. *Journal of Gay & Lesbian Mental Health, 18,* 95–109.

Dilley, P. (2002). *Queer man on campus: A history of non-heterosexual men in college, 1945–2000.* New York: RoutledgeFalmer.

Ghaziani, A. (2011). Post-gay collective identity construction. *Social Problems, 58,* 99–125.

Gillborn, D. (2005). Education policy as an act of white supremacy: Whiteness, critical race theory and education reform. *Journal of Education Policy, 20*(4), 485–505.

Giroux, H. (2002). Neoliberalism, corporate culture, and the promise of higher education: The university as a democratic public sphere. *Harvard Educational Review, 72*(4), 425–464.

Godard, B. J., Mukjerjee, A. P., & Mukherjee, A. (2006). Translating minoritized cultures: Issues of caste, class and gender. *Postcolonial Text, 2*(3), 1–23.

Herdt, G. (2013). *Gay and lesbian youth*. New York: Routledge.

Johnson, D. M., & Fox, J. A. (2003). Creating curb cuts in the classroom: Adapting universal design principles to higher education. In J. L. Higbee (Ed.) *Curriculum transformation and disability: Implementing universal design in higher education* (pp. 7–22). Minneapolis, MN: Center for Research on Developmental Education and Urban Literacy.

Johnson, J., & Amella, E. J. (2014). Isolation of lesbian, gay, bisexual and transgender youth: A dimensional concept analysis. *Journal of Advanced Nursing, 70*, 523–532.

Kelly, K. (2014). Fostering inclusion for universal design for learning. *Diversity & Democracy. 17*(4).

Keuroghlian, A. S., Shtasel, D., & Bassuk, E. L. (2014). Out on the street: A public health and policy agenda for lesbian, gay, bisexual, and transgender youth who are homeless. *American Journal of Orthopsychiatry, 84*, 66–72.

Kezar, A. (2012). *Embracing non-tenure track faculty: Changing campuses for the new faculty majority*. New York: Routledge.

Killerman, S. (2013). *The social justice advocate's handbook: A guide to gender*. Austin, TX: Impetus Books.

Kosciw, J. G., Greytak, E. A., Palmer, N. A., & Boesen, M. J. (2014). *The 2013 National School Climate Survey: The experiences of lesbian, gay, bisexual and transgender youth in our nation's schools*. New York, NY: GLSEN.

Liu, R. T., & Mutanski, B. (2012). Suicidal ideation and self-harm in lesbian, gay, bisexual, and transgender youth. *American Journal of Preventive Medicine, 42*(3), 221–228.

Marine, S. (2011). Special issue: Stonewall's legacy–bisexual, gay, lesbian, and transgender students in higher education. [*ASHE Higher Education Report, 37*(4)]. San Francisco, CA: Jossey-Bass.

Marine, S. B., & Nicolazzo, Z. (2014). Names that matter: Exploring the tensions of campus LGBTQ centers and trans* inclusion. *Journal of Diversity in Higher Education, 7*, 265–281.

McAleavey, A. A., Castonguay, L. G., & Locke, B. D. (2011). Sexual orientation minorities in college counseling: Prevalence, distress, and symptom profiles. *Journal of College Counseling, 14*, 127–142.

Miller, N. (1995). *Out of the past: Gay and lesbian history from 1869 to the present*. New York, NY: Random House.

Nguyen, D., Gonyo, C., Brazelton, G. B., Long, L. D., Secrist, S., Renn, K. A., et al. (2014, November). *Peers as sources of support to LGBTQ students*. Presented at the Annual Meeting of the Association for the Study of Higher Education, Washington, DC.

Obear, K. (2013). How to be an ally: Things to keep in mind. Presentation handouts of K. Obear, available from author.

Patton, L. D., Harper, S. R., & Harris, J. (2015). Using critical race theory to (re)interpret widely studied topics related to U.S. higher education. In A. M. Martinez-Alemán, B. Pusser, & E. M. Bensimon (Eds.), *Critical approaches to the study of higher education: A practical introduction* (pp. 193–219). Baltimore, MD: Johns Hopkins University.

Patton, L., Kortegast, C., & Javier, G. (2011). LGBTQ millennials in college. In F. Bonner, A. Marbley, & M. Howard-Hamilton, (Eds.), (*Diverse millennial students in college: Implications for faculty and student affairs* (pp. 175–192). Herndon, VA: Stylus Publishing.

Patton, L. D., Renn, K. A., Guido, F. M., & Quaye, S. J. (2016). *Student development in college: Theory, research, and practice* (3rd ed.). San Francisco, Jossey-Bass.

Peña-Talamantes, A. E. (2013). Empowering the self, creating worlds: Lesbian and gay Latina/o college students' identity negotiation in figured worlds. *Journal of College Student Development, 54*, 267–282.

Rankin, S. R., Weber, G., Blumenfeld, W., Frazer, M. S., & Pride, C. (2010). *2010 state of higher education for LGBT people.* Charlotte, NC: Campus Pride.

Renn, K. A., & Reason, R. D. (2013). *College students in the United States: Characteristics, experiences, and outcomes.* San Francisco, CA: Jossey-Bass.

Rowe, M. 2008. Micro-affirmations and micro-inequities. *Journal of the International Ombudsman Association, 1*(1).

Russell, S. T., Clarke, T. J., & Clary, J. (2009). Are teens "post-gay"?: Contemporary adolescents' sexual identity labels. *Journal of Youth and Adolescence, 38,* 884–890.

Russon, J. M., & Schmidt, C. K. (2014). Authenticity and career decision-making self-efficacy in lesbian, gay, and bisexual college students. *Journal of Gay & Lesbian Social Services, 26,* 207–221.

Sanlo, R. L., Rankin, S., & Schoenberg, R. (2002). *Our place on campus: Lesbian, gay, bisexual, transgender services and programs in higher education.* Westport, CT: Greenwood Press.

Seidman, S. (2004). *Beyond the closet: The transformation of gay and lesbian life.* New York, NY: Routledge.

Sue, D. W., Capodilupo, C. M., Torino, G. C., Bucceri, J. M., Holder, A. M. B., Nadal, K., & Esquilin, M. (2007). Racial microaggressions in everyday life: Implications for clinical practice. *American Psychologist, 62,* 271–286.

Swank, E., & Fahs, B. (2012). Resources, social networks, and collective action frames of college students who join the gay and lesbian rights movement. *Journal of Homosexuality, 59,* 67–89.

Tompkins, A. (2014). Asterisk. *Transgender Studies Quarterly, 1*(1–2), 26–27.

Vaccaro, A. (2012). Campus microclimates for LGBT faculty, staff, and students: An exploration of the intersections of social identity and campus roles. *Journal of Student Affairs Research and Practice, 49,* 429–446.

Vaid, U. (1995). *Virtual equality: The mainstreaming of gay & lesbian liberation.* New York, NY: Anchor Books.

Woodford, M., & Kulick, A. (2014) Academic and social integration on campus among sexual minority students: The impacts of psychological and experiential campus climate. *American Journal of Community Psychology, 55,* 3–24.

Woodford, M. R., Howell, M. L., Silverschanz, P., & Yu, L. (2012). "That's so gay!": Examining the covariates of hearing this expression among gay, lesbian, and bisexual college students. *Journal of American College Health, 60,* 429–434.

DEBRA BAZARSKY *is the director of the Lesbian, Gay, Bisexual, and Transgender Center at Princeton University.*

LESLIE K. MORROW *is the director of the LGBT Resource Center at the University of Illinois at Urbana-Champaign.*

GABRIEL C. JAVIER *is assistant dean of students and director of the LGBT Campus Center at the University of Wisconsin-Madison.*

NEW DIRECTIONS FOR STUDENT SERVICES • DOI: 10.1002/ss

This chapter offers both challenges and new directions in conducting quantitative assessments and research with queer-spectrum and trans-spectrum college student populations. Both the challenges and future directions are grounded in the literature and the experiences of the authors.

Identifying, Quantifying, and Operationalizing Queer-Spectrum and Trans-Spectrum Students: Assessment and Research in Student Affairs

Susan (Sue) Rankin, Jason C. Garvey

Perhaps nowhere is the expression "the only constant is change" more evident than in student affairs. The experiences of college students are ever changing, which means that student affairs professionals have to recognize and act on these changes or they will quickly find themselves left behind. Those of us who conduct assessments with students who identify within the queer-spectrum[1] (bisexual, gay, lesbian, queer, pansexual, same-gender loving, etc.) and/or the trans-spectrum (androgynous, gender nonconforming, genderqueer, transfeminine, transmasculine, transgender, etc.) can attest to the extensive changes within this community just in the last decade.

In this chapter, we offer both challenges and new directions in conducting quantitative assessments and research with queer-spectrum and transspectrum college student populations. Both the challenges and future directions are grounded in the literature and the experiences of the authors.

---

[1]Given the fluid and evolving sexual and gender identities of individuals, we use the terms *queer*-spectrum and *trans*-spectrum to value how individuals choose to identify themselves as opposed to placing them into socially constructed, fixed categories of sexuality and gender. That said, in the majority of the literature examining sexual identity and gender identity, researchers use the acronym "LGBT" to reference sexual and gender minorities. Our paradigm suggests that sexual identities and gender identities are fluid. We feel it is important to value individual identities, as opposed to placing people into fixed, socially constructed categories of sexuality or gender. In our summary of the literature offered here, we use the terminology that the authors have used in their own studies (for example, LGB, LGBT, LGBQ), whereas any synthesis and discussion adopts the queer-spectrum and trans-spectrum language.

New Directions for Student Services, no. 152, Winter 2015 © 2015 Wiley Periodicals, Inc.
Published online in Wiley Online Library (wileyonlinelibrary.com) • DOI: 10.1002/ss.20146

The Challenges

Methodologically, there are challenges at both the national and local levels for assessments and research for queer-spectrum and trans-spectrum college students. The following section outlines the current dilemmas for quantitative data collection and use among queer-spectrum and trans-spectrum college students.

Lack of Inclusion in National Datasets.   Social identities are fundamentally important within student affairs research and assessment, yet there are few established guidelines for contextualizing demographic variables into empirical analyses, particularly within quantitative research. Within the field of student affairs, there are a select number of national datasets that provide a strong foundation for innovative empirical analyses. Although these national quantitative datasets heavily influence research and practice, scholarly communities do not have a holistic or transparent understanding of how participant information is collected. Garvey (2014) conducted a study to identify higher education and student affairs survey instruments that were used in analyses for three or more studies published in tier-one journals from 2010 to 2012. Findings from his study demonstrate the high prevalence and use of certain higher education and student affairs survey instruments. Of the 10 most widely used survey instruments, only 4 asked about sexual identity and 2 included transgender identity.

Garvey (2014) also found that among the 373 quantitative studies published in tier-one journals from 2010 to 2012, only 7 (1.88%) included sexual identity and 2 (0.54%) included transgender identity. The only tier-one higher education and student affairs journal to publish quantitative articles with sexual and transgender identity was the *Journal of College Student Development*.

The general omission of sexual and transgender identities in quantitative research is highly problematic. These findings are astonishing and unacceptable given the importance of quantitative scholarship in advancing institutional, state, and national policies in higher education and student affairs (Stage, 2007). Unfortunately, because of the subject and content of quantitative analyses, these journals are in essence erasing the experiences of queer-spectrum and trans-spectrum people. Consequently, institutional advocacy, policy reform, and resource allocation are all hindered by the absence of quantitative studies that closely examine these populations.

Lack of Inclusion on Institutional Forms.   On a more local level, campuses are just starting to grapple with the addition of sexual identity and gender identity on institutional forms. (For a more detailed review, please refer to Vaccaro, Russell, and Koob in this volume). Elmhurst College's recent decision to add sexual orientation to its admission's application (Elmhurst College, 2012, p. 3) influenced other schools to take notice. In 2012, the University of Iowa became the first public university to include a question about sexual orientation and gender identity on its application

NEW DIRECTIONS FOR STUDENT SERVICES • DOI: 10.1002/ss

(Hoover, 2012), and at the University of Pennsylvania, admissions officers now examine essays for evidence of applicants' sexual orientation (Steinberg, 2010; Young, 2011). At the University of California and California State University, however, administrators are still deliberating whether or not to adopt the practice (Gordon, 2012). Aside from these developments, the Common Application—a national organization representing a few hundred schools and their admissions processes—recently chose not to include a demographic for sexual orientation and gender identity, reasoning that "colleges have other ways to indicate support for applicants who are gay or who do [not] identify with traditional gender categories, and that adding the questions could pose problems" (Jaschik, 2011, para. 1).

The Common Application may have issued its decision after considering a few noteworthy reservations: Could this kind of demographic harm queer-spectrum and trans-spectrum students, perhaps "outing" them to homophobic administrators, faculty members, and fellow students—or even to unsuspecting parents? Could confidential information accidentally enter the public realm, despite clear legal restrictions from the Family Educational Rights and Privacy Act (1974), also known as FERPA? Or could institutions overlook more fundamental concerns for queer-spectrum and trans-spectrum students, such as homophobia, marginalization, stigmatization, and discrimination?

Hundreds of institutions serve queer-spectrum and trans-spectrum students via outreach programs delivered through offices with names like LGBT Life, LGBT Resource Center, and Campus Pride Center. These offices regularly advance the following objectives: to address and respond to homophobia within the campus community, to educate the campus's various stakeholders about queer-spectrum and trans-spectrum issues, to foster diversity, and to provide a sense of community. Outreach programs also ensure that students receive the benefits of educational best practices—those kinds of personalized services that promote learning, scholarship, friendship, self-potential, and self-actualization—and make any campus a safer, less-discriminatory place (Marine, 2011a, 2011b; Sanlo, Rankin, & Schoenberg, 2002).

Although queer-spectrum and trans-spectrum outreach services are relatively common within academe, very few institutions have considered Elmhurst's approach—that is, to identify queer-spectrum and trans-spectrum students *before* arriving on campus. According to Jaschik (2010), the admissions process and retention efforts forge a complementary relationship: "Colleges use demographic information to reach out to students— before admissions decisions have been made—to tell them about programs and services for various group" (para. 9). By mining demographic data during the admissions process, institutions are able to connect students with various on-campus organizations, like religious and cultural groups, and to develop a better understanding of their student body. Thus, any student who identifies as lesbian, gay, bisexual, or transgender while filling out an application could subsequently receive queer-spectrum and trans-spectrum materials from the institution. The chief diversity officer at the University of Iowa explains how the practice works:

> What we've heard from students, especially LGBT students, is that they don't find out about support services and organizations until they've been here for a year or two. [Sending out LGBT information after receiving an application] allows us to [increase our] personal outreach. (Hoover, 2012, para. 8)

Outreach programs that connect other marginalized populations to critical extra-curricular services (for example, cultural organizations, spiritual groups, and others) have generated positive results (Adams, 2012; Johnson, Takesue, & Chen, 2007; Schmidt, 2009) as have those programs that address queer-spectrum and trans-spectrum students of color and other intersectional identities (Abes, 2012; Patton, Shahjahan, & Osei-Kofi, 2010; Poynter & Washington, 2005; Schueler, Hoffman, & Peterson, 2013). Any institution that seeks to quantify sexual identity and gender identity, some would argue, is behaving in a similar fashion: It is simply trying to connect LGBT students to the campus community at large and to track their academic progress from matriculation through graduation (Baum, 2012; Ceglar, 2012; Newhouse, 2013).

A New Landscape: Emerging Methodological Considerations

The following section outlines and discusses potential methodological considerations for including social identities in quantitative analyses focusing on queer-spectrum and trans-spectrum students. We specifically discuss experiential versus outcome assessments and assessment question inclusion and format. We also call for assessments with theoretical foundations in queer theory and intersectionality.

Experiential Assessments Versus Outcome Assessments.   According to Pascarella and Terenzini (2005), involvement, engagement, and affiliation are central to students' development and progress in college. The cocurricular nature of these experiences is the purview of student affairs professionals. Students' educational success is strongly influenced by the "context of and attitude toward their education . . . including their sense of school and social 'inclusion' and 'exclusion'" (Silverschanz, Cortina, Konik, & Magley, 2008, p. 181). Because development associated with the college years has far-reaching implications for students' lives, it is imperative that barriers to personal development are addressed for LGBT college students (Sorgen, 2011).

In a recent review of LGBTQ research in higher education, Renn (2010) identified three strands of LGBTQ scholarship: visibility, campus climate, and identity and experiences. Until recently, the majority of the assessments and research focused on the experiences of queer-spectrum and trans-spectrum students in regard to these three strands. Three decades of assessments suggested that the experiences for queer-spectrum and trans-spectrum students were similar across a number of institutions and included harassment, fears for physical safety; derogatory remarks or jokes; anti-LGBT graffiti; stereotyping by students; limited or lack of LGBT role models or access to support services; censorship in classroom environment for fear of negative consequences; exclusion of sexual identity into curriculum; and a lack of institutional policies that incorporate queer-spectrum and trans-spectrum issues or limited awareness of such policies when they are in existence (for a comprehensive review, the reader is directed to Marine, 2011b and Rankin, Weber, Blumenfeld, & Frazer, 2010). Hill and Grace (2009) suggested that the U.S. academic environment promulgates a dominant heteronormative culture.

Assessments focusing on queer-spectrum and trans-spectrum student outcomes were less prevalent in the literature, but a few studies were offered. For example, Silverschanz et al. (2008) examined the associations between heterosexist harassment and academic and psychological well-being, and Rankin et al. (2010) examined how campus climate influenced queer-spectrum and trans-spectrum students' intent to persist.

More recent literature on queer-spectrum and trans-spectrum populations has started to focus on specific outcome measures (for example, resiliency,[2] health & well-being,[3] suicidality,[4] academic success,[5] level of outness[6]) but few of these studies focus specifically on college students. We contend that outcome-based assessments should be the future of queer-spectrum and trans-spectrum student assessments. These assessments should consider who we name as queer-spectrum and trans-spectrum students, focus on the multiple and intersecting identities of queer-spectrum and trans-spectrum students, and provide theoretical underpinnings for the study of queer-spectrum and trans-spectrum students.

Naming Who We Are: Question Inclusion and Format. There are a plethora of social identities that researchers may include and focus upon in quantitative analyses. These demographic variables may include the following: gender identity/performance (including trans∗ identities[7]),

---

[2]Button, O'Connell, & Gealt (2012); Nicolazzo (2015).
[3]Feinstein, Goldfried, & Davila (2012); Haas et al. (2010); Woodford, Krentzman, & Gattis (2012).
[4]Mustanski & Liu (2013); Newcomb, Heinz, & Mustanski (2012).
[5]Garvey & Rankin (in press); Rankin et al. (2011); Sorgen (2011).
[6]Garvey & Rankin (2015); Sorgen (2011).
[7]As explained by T.J. Jourian in his chapter in this volume, "The asterisk at the end of the prefix trans is used to signal broad inclusivity of multiple gender identities beyond just trans men (also referred to as female-to-male or transgender men) or trans women (also referred to as male-to-female or transgender women), such as nonbinary individuals, as well as crossdressers and even gender performers like drag kings and queens (Tompkins, 2014)."

race/ethnicity, age, socioeconomic status, immigration status/nationality, religion/spirituality, sexual identity, and ability, among others (Adams et al., 2013). Before delving into question inclusion and format, it is important to first consider the population a researcher is studying. When distributing a survey to an entire population of individuals (for example, undergraduate students, faculty and staff, college and university alumni), a researcher must consider the identity salience of all participants. As there is no underlying social identity connection between research participants when conducting an all-population study, it is most appropriate to include questions across all social identities (Garvey, 2014). Abes, Jones, and McEwen's (2007) Model of Multiple Dimensions of Identity is a useful tool for scholars as they consider the importance of identity salience and contextual influences in social identities as lenses through which participants experience their environments. Although one individual may have a high identity salience for one particular aspect of his/her/hir/their experience, there are many others who may experience the same experience through the lens of a different social identity.

Consequently, scholars must not prioritize certain social identities while simultaneously ignoring others. It is for this reason that survey methodologists must examine the entire lived experiences of their participants to fully capture their complexities across numerous social identities. As discussed earlier, though, there is a general omission of certain social identities in current higher education and student affairs research for broad population studies. As a scholarly community, we find ourselves in a catch-22, whereby certain social identities are underresearched, yet survey developers do not include these demographic questions because of a lack of empirical research on these populations. One such community that is relatively underrepresented in general population higher education and student affairs surveys is queer-spectrum and trans-spectrum students.

When studying a specific community (for example, student veterans, international faculty), a researcher must consider the identity salience and connectivity of the sample population. What social identity or identities connect this group of individuals to form a shared experience and/or identity? Whereas it is still essential to capture individuals' multiple dimensions of identity (Abes et al., 2007), there is likely an underlying shared identity and/or experience that aligns research participants when examining a specific community. It may be appropriate to pay special attention to these connecting social identities and experiences when conducting within-community research.

When researching queer-spectrum and trans-spectrum individuals, most scholars consider only sexual identity (for example, gay, lesbian, bisexual) and sometimes gender identity (man, woman, trans∗). However, there are numerous other social identity classifications that capture a different and more nuanced aspect of a person's identity. For broad population studies, it may be adequate to include only sexual and gender identities in survey design. For queer-spectrum and trans-spectrum-specific studies,

Table 5.1. Sexual Identity Questions on Survey Designs

The Williams Institute (2009)	*Rankin et al. (2010)*
Do you consider yourself to be: heterosexual or straight; gay or lesbian; or bisexual?	What is your current sexual identity? Please mark all that apply: Asexual Bisexual Gay Heterosexual Lesbian Man loving man/MSM Pansexual Queer Questioning Woman loving woman/WSW Other (please specify) _____

scholars may consider including other social identity categories to capture a more nuanced understanding of these individuals. Such social identity classifications may include sexual identity, sexual behavior, sexual attraction, gender identity, gender performance, and/or assigned birth sex. For a more detailed operationalization of these social identities, please refer to the Williams Institute's reports on sexual orientation (Badgett & Goldberg, 2009) and gender-related measures (Herman, 2014) in survey designs.

The ways in which scholars ask about specific social identities may also vary vastly when conducting a full population study versus study with only queer-spectrum and trans-spectrum students. Consider the following example to understand the advantages and disadvantages of focusing on a specific identity community. Both questions ask participants about sexual identity, yet one focuses on an entire population sample and the other on queer-spectrum and trans-spectrum individuals only. Table 5.1 outlines two methods scholars have used to ask about sexual identity on survey designs. Items on the left side are recommendations from the Williams Institute (2009) for an entire population, and items on the right are examples from Rankin et al. (2010) that examined the experiences of LGBTQ people in higher education.

What are the evident differences between the two questions? First, there are far fewer response options for the Williams Institute's (2009) item. Rankin and colleagues' (2010) question responses include 11 different options, and there are still many other sexual identities that are not included in these response options (thus the inclusion of "other" as a response choice). The Williams Institute (2009) included only three response options. As discussed previously, there are specific differences in functionality for these two items. The Williams Institute (2009) recommends the inclusion of these items in an all-population study. Although there are likely gay, lesbian, and bisexual individuals in these samples, they do not constitute a majority of the respondents' salient identities. It is therefore not as necessary to offer an inclusive list of sexual identities because most individuals in the population do not identify as a sexual identity minority. In contrast, Rankin and colleagues (2010) surveyed only queer-spectrum and trans-spectrum individuals. The diversity of sexual identities is likely much more vast with this community-specific sample, thus justifying the inclusion of many more identity options.

Second, Rankin and colleagues' (2010) response includes a category that allows participants to write in an alternative response option that is not listed. By allowing participants to write in their own identities, it removes the necessity to prescribe a person's sexual identity. Additionally, Rankin and colleagues allow respondents to select more than one sexual identity. For example, an individual may check both bisexual and fluid or lesbian and queer. Identities are complicated and nonfixed (Abes et al., 2007); including multiple response options celebrates the messiness of social identities.

In summary, reform in student affairs assessment and research requires a reconsideration of survey question inclusion and format. Such changes may enable a more fluid and dynamic understanding of queer-spectrum and trans-spectrum students. Continuing this conversation of fluid and evolving social identities, researchers must also examine theoretical underpinnings and frameworks for examining queer-spectrum and trans-spectrum students. Queer theory and intersectionality are two theoretical frameworks that we offer for consideration in student affairs assessment and research.

Queer Theory.   Allowing individuals to prescribe their own identity and select more than one identity adheres to a more fluid and nonbinary understanding of social identities. Queer theory (Tierney & Dilley, 1996) challenges assumptions of sexual and gender normalcy and deviancy that have historically privileged some and silenced others. Many scholars who use queer theory in their research do so by dismantling identity binaries. Queer theory suspends normalized classifications to encompass a more social, fluid, and multiple understanding of identity (Britzman, 1995; Lugg, 2003).

Although queer theory derived originally from colleges and universities, few scholars in postsecondary disciplines have utilized queer tenets in research. Recently, scholars have called for the increased use of queer theory as a lens to examine higher education and student affairs issues and individuals. Using critical queer ideals in quantitative research adds to the depth of higher education and student affairs scholarship, as well as advances the methods and ideals for research on queer-spectrum and trans-spectrum students. In her seminal article examining queer theory uses in higher education and student affairs research, Renn (2010) wrote, "I call for increased use of queer theory and new research approaches at the same time that I call for continuation of large-scale studies" (p. 138). Survey designers may consider using queer theory to produce items that more adequately capture the fluid dynamics of social identities, particularly when studying within queer-spectrum and trans-spectrum communities.

Intersectionality. Intersectionality is a research paradigm that offers new ways to understand the complexity of social identities. Cole (2009) wrote, "Rather than prescribing—or proscribing—any particular research or data analysis technique, the concept of intersectionality entails a conceptual shift in the way researchers understand social categories" (p. 178). Developed through Black feminist thought and originally coined by Crenshaw (1991), intersectionality refers to the interaction between gender, race, and other categories of difference and the outcomes of these interactions as they relate to power. Intersectionality encourages scholars to understand how systems of oppression intersect to create structures, political systems, and cultural contexts that shape the experiences of individuals with oppressed identities. More specifically, intersectional scholars are interested in the relationships among social groups defined by the inclusion of all groups in each social category (McCall, 2005).

McCall (2005) provided commentary on intersectionality from a methodological standpoint. She discussed that there are no established guidelines for empirically addressing research questions informed by an intersectional framework and recognized that the current restriction on intersectional research comes down primarily to methods. Although a large portion of intersectional work employs qualitative methods, intersectional theorists must use quantitative techniques to advance intersectionality as a research paradigm. Dubrow (2008) wrote that "[w]e need to stop wondering whether quantitative analysis of survey data is appropriate for accounting for intersectionality. The challenge now is to strengthen the bond between intersectionality theory and quantitative techniques" (p. 99).

Intersectionality offers researchers new ways to operationalize complex social identities. Survey methodologists can modify demographic collection and analytic techniques to facilitate more intersectional research. Dubrow (2008) discussed that for quantitative scholars who want to incorporate intersectional theory with existing survey data, interaction terms are an appropriate way to measure relationships among social identities. Similarly, McCall (2005) advocated for a research design with demographic information as independent variables with main effects and interactions. She termed this technique as the categorical approach to intersectionality, "focus[ing] on the complexity of relationships among multiple social groups within and across analytical categories . . . . The subject is multigroup and the method is systematically comparative" (p. 1786). Multiple categories analyze intersections of demographics and categories within, simultaneously examining power and privilege in relation to social identities.

Concluding Thoughts

Regarding higher education and student affairs research, Stage (2007) described two broad tasks for quantitative scholars. First, researchers should use data to represent and uncover large-scale processes and outcomes that perpetuate systemic social or institutional inequities. Second, scholars must question quantitative models, measures, and analytic practices in order to propose competing models, measures, and analytic practices that more appropriately describe minority individuals and communities. Quantitative scholars should reflect upon using the aforementioned emerging methodological considerations in order to achieve these tasks set forth by Stage. In doing so, they may provide a more nuanced understanding of demographic variables and recognize the complexity and evolving nature of queer-spectrum and trans-spectrum individuals.

References

Abes, E. S. (2012). Constructivist and intersectional interpretations of a lesbian college student's multiple social identities. *Journal of Higher Education, 83*(2), 186–216.

Abes, E. S., Jones, S. R., & McEwen, M. K. (2007). Reconceptualizing the model of Multiple dimensions of identity: The role of meaning-making capacity in the construction of multiple identities. *Journal of College Student Development, 48*(1), 1–22. doi: 10.1353/csd.2007.0000

Adams, C. (2012). College remains elusive goal for many Latino students. *Education Week, 31*(34), 16–19.

Adams, M., Blumenfeld, W. J., Castaneda, C., Hackman, H., Peters, M., & Zuniga X. (Eds.). (2013). *Readings for diversity and social justice* (2nd ed.). New York, NY: Routledge.

Badgett, L., & Goldberg, N. (Eds.). (2009). *Best practices for asking questions about sexual orientation on surveys*. Created by the Sexual Minority Assessment Research Team (SMART). Los Angeles, CA: The Williams Institute.

Baum, B. S. (2012, Fall). LGBT applicants and challenges for admission: Five cases. *Journal of College Admission*, 25–29.

Britzman, D. P. (1995). Is there a queer pedagogy? Or, stop reading straight. *Educational Theory, 45*, 151–165.

Button, D. M., O'Connell, D. J., & Gealt, R. (2012). Sexual minority youth victimization and social support: The intersection of sexuality, gender, race, and victimization. *Journal of Homosexuality, 59*(1), 18–43.

Ceglar, T. (2012, Spring). Targeted recruitment of GLBT students by colleges and universities. *Journal of College Admission*, 18–23.

Cole, E. R. (2009). Intersectionality and research in psychology. *American Psychologist, 64*, 170–180.

Crenshaw, K. (1991). Mapping the margins: Intersectionality, identity politics, and violence against women of color. *Stanford Law Review, 43*, 1241–1299.

Dubrow, J. K. (2008). How can we account for intersectionality in quantitative analysis of survey data? *Empirical illustration for Central and Eastern Europe. ASK, 17*, 85–100.

Elmhurst College. (2012). *Application for admission*. Retrieved from http://media.elmhurst.edu/documents/Elmhurst_Application_2012.pdf.

Family Educational Rights and Privacy Act, 20 U.S.C. § 1232g C.F.R. (1974).

Feinstein, B. A., Goldfried, M. R., & Davila, J. (2012). The relationship between experiences of discrimination and mental health among lesbians and gay men: An examination of internalized homonegativity and rejection sensitivity as potential mechanisms. *Journal of Consulting and Clinical Psychology, 80*(5), 917.

Garvey, J. (2014). Demographic information collection in higher education and student affairs survey instruments: Developing a national landscape for intersectionality. In C. S. D. Mitchell, & L. Greyerbiehl (Eds.), *Intersectionality and higher education: Research, theory, and praxis* (pp. 201–216). New York, NY: Peter Lang.

Garvey, J., & Rankin, S. (2015). The influence of campus experiences on the level of out-ness among trans-spectrum and queer-spectrum students. *Journal of Homosexuality*, 62, 374–393.

Garvey, J., & Rankin, S. (in press). Making the grade? Examining the classroom climate for queer spectrum and trans-spectrum students. *Journal of Student Affairs Research and Practice*.

Gordon, L. (2012, March 30). California state colleges weigh asking students about sexual orientation. *Los Angeles Times*. Retrieved from http://articles.latimes.com/2012/mar/30/local/la-me-uc-gay-20120330.

Haas, A. P., Eliason, M., Mays, V. M., Mathy, R. M., Cochran, S. D., D'Augelli, A. R., et al. (2010). Suicide and suicide risk in lesbian, gay, bisexual, and transgender populations: Review and recommendations. *Journal of Homosexuality*, 58(1), 10–51.

Herman, J. L. (Ed.) (2014). *Best practices for asking questions to identify transgender and other gender minority respondents on population-based surveys*. Created by the Gender Identity in U.S. Surveillance (GenIUSS) Group. Los Angeles, CA: The Williams Institute.

Hill, R. J., & Grace, A. P. (2009). *Adult and higher education in queer contexts: Power, politics, and pedagogy*. Chicago: Discovery Association Publishing House.

Hoover, E. (2012, December 12). University of Iowa will ask applicants if they identify with gay community. *The Chronicle of Higher Education*, p. 11.

Jaschik, S. (2010, August 12). Asking more than male or female. *Inside Higher Education*. Retrieved from http://www.insidehighered.com/news/2010/08/12/questions.

Jaschik, S. (2011, January 26). The same boxes to check. *Inside Higher Ed*. Retrieved from http://www.insidehighered.com/news/2011/01/26/common_application_rejects_new_questions_on_sexual_orientation_and_gender_identity.

Johnson, A. B., Takesue, K., & Chen, B. (2007). Identity-based discussion groups: A means of providing outreach and support for Asian Pacific American students. *Journal of College Counseling*, 10(2), 184–192.

Lugg, C. A. (2003). Sissies, faggots, lezzies, and dykes: Gender, sexual orientation, and a new politics of education? *Educational Administration Quarterly*, 39(1), 95–134.

Marine, S. B. (2011a). *Stonewall's legacy: Bisexual, gay, lesbian, and transgender students in higher education*. Hoboken, NJ: Wiley Periodicals.

Marine, S. B. (2011b). Stonewall's legacy: Bisexual, gay, lesbian, and transgender student in higher education. [*ASHE Higher Education Report*, 37(4)]. San Francisco, CA: Jossey-Bass.

McCall, L. (2005). The complexity of intersectionality. *Signs*, 30, 1771–1800.

Mustanski, B., & Liu, R. T. (2013). A longitudinal study of predictors of suicide at-tempts among lesbian, gay, bisexual, and transgender youth. *Archives of Sexual Behavior*, 42(3), 437–448.

Newcomb, M. E., Heinz, A. J., & Mustanski, B. (2012). Examining risk and protective factors for alcohol use in lesbian, gay, bisexual, and transgender youth: a longitudinal multilevel analysis. *Journal of Studies on Alcohol and Drugs*, 73(5), 783.

Newhouse, M. R. (2013, Summer). Remembering the "T" in LGBT: Recruiting and sup-porting transgender students. *Journal of College Admission*, 22–27.

Nicolazzo, Z. (2015). *"Just go in looking good": The resilience, resistance, and kinship-building of trans* college students*. Unpublished doctoral dissertation, Miami University.

Pascarella, E. T., & Terenzini, P. T. (2005). *How college affects students: A third decade of research* (Vol. 2). San Francisco, CA: Jossey-Bass.

Patton, L. D., Shahjahan, R. A., & Osei-Kofi, N. (2010). Introduction to the emergent approaches to diversity and social justice in higher education special issue. *Equity & Excellence in Education*, 43(3), 265–278. doi: 10.1080/10665684.2010.496692

Poynter, K. J., & Washington, J. (2005). Multiple identities: Creating community on campus for LGBT students. In R. L. Sanlo (Ed.), *New Directions for Student Services:*

No. 111. Gender identity and sexual orientation: Research, policy, and personal perspectives (pp. 41–47). San Francisco, CA: Jossey-Bass.

Rankin, S., Merson, D., Sorgen, C., McHale, I., Loya, K., & Oseguera, L. (2011). *Student-Athlete Climate Study (SACS) final report*. University Park, PA: The Pennsylvania State University.

Rankin, S., Weber, G., Blumenfeld, W., & Frazer, S. (2010). *2010 state of higher education for lesbian, gay, bisexual & transgender people*. Charlotte, NC: Campus Pride.

Renn, K. A. (2010). LGBT and queer research in higher education: The state and status of the field. *Educational Researcher, 39*(2), 10. doi: doi:10.3102/0013189×10362579

Sanlo, R., Rankin, S., & Schoenberg, R. (2002). *Our place on campus: Lesbian, gay, bisexual, and transgender services and programs in higher education*. Westport, CT: Greenwood Press.

Schmidt, P. (2009). Colleges seek key to success of black men in the classroom. *Education Digest* (7), 4.

Schueler, L. A., Hoffman, J. A., & Peterson, E. (2013). Fostering safe, engaging campuses for lesbian, gay, bisexual, transgender, and questioning students. In S. R. Harper & S. J. Quaye (Eds.), *Student engagement in higher education* (pp. 61–80). New York, NY: Routledge.

Silverschanz, P., Cortina, L., Konik, J., & Magley, V. (2008). Slurs, snubs, and queer jokes: Incidence and impact of heterosexist harassment in academia. *Sex Roles, 58*(3–4), 179–191. doi: 10.1007/s11199-007-9329-7

Sorgen, C. H. (2011). *The influence of sexual identity on higher education outcomes*. Doctoral dissertation, Pennsylvania State University. Retrieved from https://etda.libraries.psu.edu/paper/12180.

Stage, F. K. (2007). Answering critical questions using quantitative data. In F. K. Stage (Ed.), *New Directions for Institutional Research: No. 133. Using quantitative data to answer critical questions* (pp. 5–16). San Francisco, CA: Jossey-Bass.

Steinberg, J. (2010, February 26). University of Pennsylvania tries outreach based on sexual orientation. *The New York Times*. Retrieved from http://thechoice.blogs.nytimes.com/2010/02/26/penn/.

Tierney, W. G., & Dilley, P. (1996). Constructing knowledge: Educational research and gay and lesbian studies. In W. Pinar (Ed.), *Queer theory in education*. Princeton, New Jersey: Lawrence Erlbaum Publishing.

Tompkins, A. (2014). Asterisk. *Transgender Studies Quarterly, 1*(1–2), 26–27.

Woodford, M. R., Krentzman, A. R., & Gattis, M. N. (2012). Alcohol and drug use among sexual minority college students and their heterosexual counterparts: the effects of experiencing and witnessing incivility and hostility on campus. *Substance Abuse and Rehabilitation, 3*, 11–23.

Young, A. (2011, Winter). Gay students: The latest outreach target at many colleges. *Journal of College Admission*, 39–40.

SUSAN (SUE) RANKIN *is retired associate professor of education policy studies and senior research associate at The Pennsylvania State University and founder of Rankin and Associates.*

JASON C. GARVEY *is an assistant professor of higher education at The University of Alabama.*

6

In this chapter, the editors provide a summary of the information shared in this sourcebook about the success of students who have minoritized identities of sexuality or gender and offer recommendations for policy, practice, and further research.

Recommendations

G. Blue Brazelton, Kristen A. Renn, Dafina-Lazarus Stewart

This sourcebook and the contributions of its authors significantly enhance the scholarship on the experiences of students who have marginalized identities of sexuality and/or gender (MIoSG; Vaccaro, Russell, & Koob, Chapter Two). We sought to establish a collection of concepts that would benefit all who serve college students with minoritized identities of sexuality and gender, by providing (a) clarity regarding and emphasizing the significance of language and identity, (b) a model for understanding minoritized identities of sexuality and gender, (c) both curricular and cocurricular considerations of the MIoSG student experience, and (d) resources for conducting meaningful research and scholarship on MIoSG college students. Considering the MIoSG student community as a large and diverse group of individuals, we also call attention to this diversity by asserting that the unique identity groups within the umbrella labels of LGBTQ or MIoSG receive specific attention whenever possible, as there is no universal experience of MIoSG college students. Note that in this volume, we have followed the increasingly common practice of an interdisciplinary community of scholars (such as Benitez, 2010; Chase, Dowd, Pazich, & Bensimon, 2014; Gillborn, 2005; Godard, Mukjerjee, & Mukherjee, 2006; Patton, Harper, & Harris, 2015) to use the term *minoritized* as we discuss those whose sexuality and gender have been consigned to lower status, visibility, and power.

Connecting the body of knowledge within this sourcebook to the work of student affairs requires specific recommendations for policy, research, and practice, representing separate threads of opportunity to provide service and support to MIoSG college students. For our recommendations, we return to the competency-based approach we used to frame this sourcebook, as we contextualize any improvements in the contexts for MIoSG college students through the positive core of opportunity and not antiquated deficit models. Affirmative and positive inquiry both requires and benefits from the collaborative scholarship of the chapter authors. Collectively, their contributions here are a collective assessment of potential avenues

NEW DIRECTIONS FOR STUDENT SERVICES, no. 152, Winter 2015 © 2015 Wiley Periodicals, Inc.
Published online in Wiley Online Library (wileyonlinelibrary.com) • DOI: 10.1002/ss.20147

of significant benefit for college students with MIoSG. Transformational change is possible through consideration of the contexts of the campus lives of students with MIoSG. This is why the authors of this sourcebook have employed an ecological perspective to understand how students with MIoSG interact with the various elements of their campus environments.

Returning to the Ecological Model

As we mentioned in the introductory chapter, an ecological understanding of college students with MIoSG and their contexts emphasizes and examines the significance of the interaction between students and campus ecologies (Renn & Arnold, 2003). The ecological model we used is an adaptation of Bronfenbrenner's (1993; Bronfenbrenner & Morris, 2006) model, which described four elements within which interactions take place: Person, Process, Context, and Time (PPCT; Renn & Arnold, 2003). By asking the authors of this volume to focus on specific interactions of students within the higher education ecological system, we hope to present a significant, yet not-comprehensive, depiction of the academic, social, and cocurricular contexts of an often studied but rarely understood student population: those within MIoSG communities.

In the first chapter, T.J. Jourian presents and examines the language around the sexually and gender minoritized communities and how the nature of sexual orientation and gender identity has both prompted change, and been changed by, various contexts, constructs, and culture. Chapter One describes MIoSG college students and communities across multiple ecological systems, such as contextualizing how an individual interacts with terminology and ideas of sexual orientation or gender identity (or both). One of Jourian's suggestions is to embrace and support debate of the term *queer* as a label for some MIoSG students or communities. The debate surrounding the term *queer* is significant and needs to be culturally and historically understood. As such, it is a useful illustration of the way students interact with the microsystems around them and, ultimately, the rest of the ecological model with which college students engage. Jourian also provides a primer for acknowledging asexual identities as a rarely acknowledged and often misunderstood identity group. Increased literacy of the language of those with sexually and gender diverse identities cultivates openness and personal and community meaning making.

Vaccaro, Russell, and Koob (Chapter Two) provide a robust model for understanding college students with minoritized identities of sexuality and gender, which also uses Bronfrenbrenner's (1993) bioecological model as an overlay for the systems and contexts students with MIoSG encounter. This second chapter presents a new model for understanding the experiences and interactions of college students with MIoSG as an understudied population in post-secondary education. We anticipate Vaccaro, Russell, and Koob's model will be used often as both a theoretical framework and a practical tool for student affairs professionals as we move forward with supporting MIoSG students and communities in higher education, given its holistic approach to the interaction of systems and contexts.

Chapters Three and Four present overviews of specific micro- and mesosystems as meaningful processes and contexts with which students with MIoSG interact in higher education: curricular, cocurricular, and general campus environments. Linley and Nguyen (Chapter Three) and Bazarsky, Morrow, and Javier (Chapter Four) show how any potential interaction between a student with MIoSG and the institutional environment represents an opportunity to influence the student's experience. Although this may appear to be common sense, the work of these scholars demonstrates the need for intentionality and mindfulness when interacting with all students, especially systematically minoritized individuals. Within curricular contexts, training faculty in sensitivity to, awareness of, and inclusivity for MIoSG can yield meaningful benefits for students, as this is the context in which academic outcomes are served (Chapter Three). Bazarsky, Morrow, and Javier (Chapter Four) affirm a similar point, that the professional staff who provide services and support to students have the same opportunity to support inclusion for or create hostile and unwelcoming climates for students with MIoSG. Both the curricular and cocurricular contexts demonstrate how students' interactions with the environment occur in some way with every level. Faculty and staff represent not only their individual roles but also their respective offices or departments, the institution, and sometimes their profession as a whole. Teaching and learning inclusivity and sensitivity is a baseline recommendation from which additional support and structure can be built to extend the arena of influence and support beyond the micro- and mesosystems into the exo- and macrosystems.

Overall, the ecological model allows for a more holistic understanding of the college student environment for MIoSG; specifically, Vaccaro, Russell, and Koob (Chapter Two) demonstrate the ecological interplay between student experiences and minoritized identities of sexuality and gender. The way in which these students interact with their environments represents how they make meaning from their experiences and ultimately affects whether or not they feel marginalized or included in their campus environments. For practitioners and scholars serving populations of college students with MIoSG, we intend for this volume and Vaccaro, Russell, and Koob's model to be useful for improving individual interactions with campus services or as a framework for creating institutional policy changes.

Recommendations

Our recommendations represent a synthesis of the scholarship of the volume's authors, and are also a reflection of the history and current status of scholarship and practice within the field of student affairs. Each of the chapters describes the evolution of research over the past decade or more, as the scholarship on college students and communities with MIoSG has matured and expanded to have significant impact on both the how and the why of the work which needs to be done. Research is the lens through which we seek to understand and inquire about the student experiences with and services to those with MIoSG. Therefore, we contend that robust scholarship on college students with MIoSG is the foundation on which student affairs should build its practice. Although we separate our recommendations into the traditional model of research, policy, and practice, these threads are intertwined with each other and should not be viewed independently.

Research. Throughout our conversations while preparing the sourcebook, we often noted that conditions are prime for undertaking new and significant research on students with MIoSG. The literature on these students and issues is developing from a young thread of research into a more robust examination of the contexts and experiences of the collegiate community of those with MIoSG. Several chapters of this volume reference the growth of this scholarship. Another goal of this sourcebook therefore is to examine the state of literature on the topic, discussing the strengths and gaps in the field's knowledge, including qualitative and quantitative scholarship, multiple philosophical perspectives, as well as a range of methodological modes of inquiry.

The use of nonbinary and gender-inclusive/flexible pronouns presents an opportunity for direct change in scholarship. By moving away from the model of traditional cisgender pronouns (for example, she and he, her and him), literature can shift the gender assumptions in writing away from genderism and cisnormativity toward a more gender-inclusive academic conversation. In Chapter One, Jourian's section of "Queering Terminology" provides a strong discussion of the role of pronouns and terms in reframing oppressive systems toward supportive language. Although nonbinary and gender-inclusive/flexible pronouns do not reflect the full diversity of identities among those who assert MIoSG, advancing such a change in scholarly writing reflects a step toward disrupting the structural exclusion of those with trans∗ [1] identities.

Researchers must also acknowledge limitations, areas of improvement, and the superficiality of some the research done regarding MIoSG. In Chapter Five, Rankin and Garvey describe multiple avenues for conducting research that can build upon the foundations that have been established without unnecessary redundancy, by employing strong quantitative methodologies as modes of inquiry, such as asking questions about

---

[1] As explained by T.J. Jourian in his chapter in this volume, "The asterisk at the end of the prefix trans is used to signal broad inclusivity of multiple gender identities beyond just trans men (also referred to as female-to-male or transgender men) or trans women (also referred to as male-to-female or transgender women), such as nonbinary individuals, as well as crossdressers and even gender performers like drag kings and queens (Tompkins, 2014)."

gender and sexual identity in inclusive ways on institutional assessments and survey instruments. These recommendations reflect a responsiveness to the lack of such student data in large datasets. It is also necessary to embrace and value scholarly critique from the community of those with MIoSG, using that criticism as opportunities to build theoretical and methodological complexity that bolster the maturation of both the research being conducted and the literature being used.

Different methodological approaches offer both opportunities and limitations to what can be examined and learned about students with MIoSG. Acknowledging the implications of these benefits and challenges helps develop the intellectual complexity we believe is beneficial to the next wave of scholarship concerning MIoSG. For instance, a qualitative methodological emphasis offers an opportunity for in-depth focus on the individuals at the focus of the research inquiry and provides a deeper understanding of the "how" and "why" of student experiences. However, qualitative methods alone are not suited for assessing systematic interactions across various domains of the experiences of students with MIoSG on campus. Qualitative methodologies, with their emphasis on depth of understanding versus breadth of representation, have greater difficulty capturing the breadth and range of within-group heterogeneity. Finally, qualitative research is generally not meant to examine causality or correlational relationships among factors related to success, resiliency, sense of belonging, and other variables of interest to scholars studying MIoSG. These limitations reinforce Rankin and Garvey's argument for stronger quantitative research, both from postpositivist and critical methodological foundations.

Another common methodological approach in research about MIoSG is the focus on identity development. Identity development research has provided foundational scholarship on MIoSG (for example, Cass, 1979; D'Augelli, 1994; Wilchins, 2002) and describes the contexts for important developmental touchstones in the lives of students with MIoSG, including identity meaning making and cognitive, moral, spiritual, and worldview development. Identity development research also recognizes the evolutionary nature of individuals' relationships to their social group memberships. However, identity development research also naturalizes identity constructions that are rooted in oppressive systems and presumes that identity is stable, that there is an end point for maturation of identity articulations, and that identity articulations are individually held and ego driven instead of performative, contextual, and fluid (Jones & Stewart, in press).

The scholarship has matured and will continue to develop through the work of many scholars who have committed themselves to understanding and describing the experiences and identities of college students with MIoSG. To support current and future scholars, we recommend building on their work with both broadened and deepened intellectual work, moving toward sophisticated inquiries across qualitative and quantitative philosophies and methodologies. In addition to the scholars who contributed to this sourcebook, other emerging and more seasoned scholars, such as Chase Catalano, Susan Marine, Z Nicolazzo, Kristie Seelman, and Dan Tillapaugh, are also among those contributing to building up a robust intellectual engagement with college students who have MIoSG. Moreover, up and coming scholars Symone Simmons and Erich Pitcher are researching MIoSG faculty and administrative/professional staff in higher education contexts. These scholars and others are using their research to promote change toward more inclusive and supportive campuses for college students with MIoSG.

Policy.   Policy discussions concerning college students with MIoSG often rest on a few touchstone issues: gender-inclusive campus facilities, protected classifications of identities, and the opportunity to have one's correct name printed on rosters and use gender-appropriate pronouns. Lack of attention to or resistance to changing these policies and practices reflects how deeply entrenched hetero- and cisgender normativity can be, whether by ignorance or willful design. Institutions can be encouraged to change policies to promote more inclusive campus climates, yet their solutions often create conditions that reify existing oppressive binaries and stereotypes. By using exclusionary language or very limited identity categories (or none at all) on institutional forms, students with MIoSG may feel unrepresented in the vision of the university or college. Even creating gender-neutral facilities, often accompanied by visual symbols of traditional genders, individuals with gender identities that are fluid or nonbinary may still not feel included in the campus environment.

On a large scale, state and national policies often defer to campuses for operationalization of inclusive and supportive practices, yet issues of inclusion and equity often remain unclarified and require a decision from a higher authoritative level. For instance, many states do not include sexual orientation or gender identity as part of their nondiscrimination clauses, resulting in the potential for a student who has a marginalized sexual or gender identity to be denied services or employment. Some states and many institutions have chosen to include sexuality and gender as protected identities within their nondiscrimination statements as a response to the ambiguity and lack of inclusion at the federal level. The U.S. landscape may change moving forward from the Supreme Court's decision in June 2015 that marriage equality is a constitutional right (*Obergefell v. Hodges*, 2015), but it is important to remember that inclusion of all people with MIoSG is not universally supported and there is still no federal legislation extending protection from discrimination on the basis of sexuality or gender identity and expression.

On college and university campuses, we recommend including gender and sexual identity topics as part of the conversation, in both the curriculum and the cocurriculum. Queer Studies (or Gender and Sexuality Studies) provide an opportunity for faculty, staff, and students to engage in the scholarship on MIoSG through the curriculum and communicates a degree of inclusion to the campus community. Our recommendation is to push past the traditional policy changes or wording that superficially promote a seemingly more inclusive environment and to transform policies and infrastructures to support the community of those with MIoSG and their complexity and diversity. The work of continuing to expect and request inclusive policies requires collaborative efforts. Students, faculty, staff, who identify with MIoSG should not be the only ones leading this charge to be responsible for their own liberation. Campus advocacy work is typically the responsibility of the MIoSG communities and its allies, an exhausting and demanding process. Those who claim to be allies must also step up as accomplices to organize for change and educate the campus community. Student affairs practitioners should refer to Vaccaro, Russell, and Koob's ecological model of students with MIoSG and campus contexts (see Chapter Two) and examine the policyscape for their institution based on type and setting in order to create a transformative strategic vision.

Practice. Specific recommendations for various arenas of practice can be found throughout the sourcebook, with particular focus on the chapters of curricular and cocurricular contexts (Chapters Three and Four). Our concluding recommendations for practice focus on broader suggestions for student affairs professionals on creating and supporting spaces, campuses, and resources beneficial and inclusive of college students with MIoSG. By making recommendations for practice, we are not attempting to direct the operation of various units within student affairs toward the adoption of best practices, such as providinggender-inclusive housing, seeking representational diversity on professional and student staffs, or suggesting programs for resource centers. Such practices actually countermand institutional transformation toward equity (Nicolazzo & Marine, 2015). However, establishing or continuing support for an MIoSG resource center resounds throughout the sourcebook as an opportunity to integrate much of the MIoSG community with the campus, yielding opportunities for additional assessment and policy change. Beyond this, we are recommending the adoption of critical philosophies and perspectives in the examination and execution of student affairs work, both by individual professionals and collectives of practitioners invested in inclusivity for college students with MIoSG. Most specifically, we argue for the rejection of the operationalization of cishetnormativity as foundational for exclusionary practice in student affairs.

Exclusionary practices exercised through cishetnormativity are harmful for students who have marginalized identities of sexuality or gender, but so are the politics and contexts of homo- and trans-normativity. At the core of these concerns is the process of assimilation and attempting to standardize and normalize the experiences of those with minoritized sexual or gender identities. Such an approach makes inclusion of the marginalized group or individual dependent on their fit with dominant norms, conditions, narratives, or limits. For example, the celebration of the Supreme Court of the United States decision for marriage equality in June 2015 is the result of presenting marriage equality as a necessary, normalizing process for gays and lesbians. Certainly, the decision is a sign of progress for the rights of monogamous couples with marginalized sexual identities, but those with nonbinary gender identities are not included in the vision and implementation of such marriage equality. Likewise, not all queer people in same-sex relationships seek to marry. Other examples include the exclusion of asexuality within discussions of sexual diversity and the fact that not all transgender and nonbinary individuals seek to use pharmaceuticals and/or surgery to effect a physical transition within a binary gender construct.

Against Best Practice.   We follow Nicolazzo's (2015) lead of arguing against "best practices." Although "best practices" are a common set of recommendations within student affairs, we argue against a generalized collection of programs and principles. At the core of the concept of "best practices" is an assumed uniform experience. The wisdom of the authors of this sourcebook, from Jourian's work on language and constructs, to Vaccaro, Russell, and Koob's holistic model of ecological contexts of MIoSG college students, to Rankin and Garvey's recommendations for deeper and more flexible scholarly inquiry, we acknowledge that there is no universal experience for college students with MIoSG.

Moreover, "best practices" create conditions that often maintain the status quo, where an environment, context, or support meant to accommodate the needs of students with MIoSG may be interpreted as sufficient. We hope this volume encourages student affairs professionals to move beyond sufficiency and toward building supportive structures for student success. The connotation and implication of the word "best" limits our practice and suggests the solution has been discovered. Nicolazzo (2015) argued against such an approach and asserted "moving beyond best practices means recognizing we always have more work we can be doing to promote gender equity and trans* inclusion" (p. 152). Best practices take an accommodating approach to queer and trans* people, which still puts them on the outside as abnormal and not included though the pretense of inclusion is there. A radical rethinking of gender and sexuality is needed and can be reflected in administrative policies that do not seek to allow accommodations or exceptions to the standard practice but create practices where to be non-standard is the presumed norm (Nicolazzo, 2015).

Continuing to work toward inclusive campuses requires difficult work, creating conditions where both systems and individuals can be transformed. For instance, instructors asking on the first day of the course for correct names on the class roster still requires trans* students to publicly disclose to the class, although a more proactive and inclusive approach would be to ask all students to sign in and then speak with the instructor after class about correct names. An improvement from waiting until the first day of class would be to contact the course participants ahead of time and ask for any updates to the roster so that the transition never occurs with other students present at all. However, a truly transformative structural shift would be to have a college or university allow students to register their correct names within the student information systems or course management software without needing to interact through some intermediary who may or may not be tolerant or accepting of trans∗ individuals. Transforming campus climates and institutional practices cannot be stagnant in light of the constantly evolving nature of MIoSG communities.

Concluding Remarks

There is significant work ahead for student affairs in creating inclusive communities and overall conditions for student success for those with MIoSG. This sourcebook may serve to reaffirm the knowledge of many scholars and practitioners. We also believe a very large proportion of student affairs professionals will benefit significantly from the contributions of the authors within this volume. Kris Renn, one of the editors of the sourcebook, has acknowledged multiple requests for glossaries of MIoSG terms by various journals when publishing findings from the National Study of LGBTQ Student Success. It is a useful reminder that not all student affairs professionals are versed in the language of support for MIoSG students, and in the absence of that knowledge, practitioners with good intentions may harm and exclude students from the services and communities they need.

We encourage those who serve college students with MIoSG to not let assumptions about these students and communities guide their practice. Our sourcebook addresses many of these assumptions and presents the realities of students with MIoSG. For instance, Linley and Nguyen include in their discussion on curricular contexts in Chapter Three that some individuals have argued how U.S. culture and politics have entered into a "post-LGBTQ" era. We argue that prematurely accepting that our society, culture, and politics have moved beyond MIoSG discrimination limits the work that needs to be done, and puts students with marginalized identities at further risk. There is still work to be done to create and sustain programs, services, campuses, and policies that support student success and inclusive communities for those with MIoSG. We are confident, however, that the scholarship of the authors of this sourcebook and other researchers provide wisdom, insight, and encouragement to accomplish this task.

References

Benitez, M. (2010). Resituating culture centers within a social justice framework: Is there room for examining whiteness? In L. Patton (Ed.), *Culture centers in higher education: Perspectives on identity, theory, and practice* (pp. 119–136). Sterling, VA: Stylus.

Bronfenbrenner, U. (1993). The ecology of cognitive development: Research models and fugitive findings. In R. H. Wozniak & K. W. Fischer (Eds.), *Development in context: Acting and thinking in specific environments* (pp. 3–44). Hillsdale, NJ: Erlbaum.

Bronfenbrenner, U., & Morris, P. A. (2006). The bioecological model of human development. In W. Damon & R. M. Lerner (Eds.), *Handbook of child psychology* (6th ed., pp. 793–828). Hoboken, NJ: Wiley.

Cass, V. C. (1979). Homosexual identity formation: A theoretical model. *Journal of Homosexuality*, 4(3), 219–235.

Chase, M. M., Dowd, A. C., Pazich, L. B., & Bensimon, E. M. (2014). Transfer equity for "minoritized" students: A critical policy analysis of seven states. *Educational Policy*, 28(5), 669–717.

D'Augelli, A. R. (1994). Identity development and sexual orientation: Toward a model of lesbian, gay, and bisexual development. In E. J. Trickett, R. J. Watts, and D. Birman (Eds.), *Human diversity: Perspectives on people in context*. San Francisco: Jossey-Bass.

Gillborn, D. (2005). Education policy as an act of white supremacy: Whiteness, critical race theory and education reform. *Journal of Education Policy*, 20(4), 485–505.

Godard, B. J., Mukjerjee, A. P., & Mukherjee, A. (2006). Translating minoritized cultures: Issues of caste, class and gender. *Postcolonial Text*, 2(3), 1–23.

Jones, S. R., & Stewart, D.-L. (in press). Evolution of student development theory. In E. S. Abes (Ed.), *New Directions for Student Services: No. XXX. Diverse and critical perspectives on student development theory* (in preparation). San Francisco, CA: Jossey-Bass.

Nicolazzo, Z. (2015). *"Just go in looking good": The resilience, resistance, and kinship-building trans∗ college students*. Unpublished doctoral dissertation, Miami University. Retrieved from https://etd.ohiolink.edu/.

Nicolazzo, Z., & Marine, S. B. (2015). "It will change if people keep talking": Trans∗ students in college and university housing. *Journal of College and University Student Housing*, 42(1), 160–177.

Obergefell v. Hodges, 576 U.S. __ (2015).

Patton, L. D., Harper, S. R., & Harris, J. (2015). Using critical race theory to (re)interpret widely studied topics related to U.S. higher education. In A. M. Martinez-Alemán, B. Pusser, & E. M. Bensimon (Eds.), *Critical approaches to the study of higher education: A practical introduction* (pp. 193–219). Baltimore, MD: Johns Hopkins University.

Renn, K. A., & Arnold, K. D. (2003). Reconceptualizing research on college student peer culture. *Journal of Higher Education*, 74(3), 261–291.

Tompkins, A. (2014). Asterisk. *Transgender Studies Quarterly*, 1(1–2), 26–27.

Wilchins, R. A. (2002). Queerer bodies. In J. Nestle, C. Howell, & R. A. Wilchins (Eds.), *Genderqueer: Voices from beyond the sexual binary*. Los Angeles, CA: Alyson.

G. BLUE BRAZELTON is assistant professor of higher education and student affairs at Northern Michigan University.

KRISTEN A. RENN is professor of higher, adult, and lifelong education at Michigan State University.

DAFINA-LAZARUS STEWART is associate professor of higher education and student affairs at Bowling Green State University.

INDEX